NOT EVERYONE GETS A TROPHY

NOT EVERYONE GETS A TROPHY

HOW TO MANAGE GENERATION Y

Bruce Tulgan

JOSSEY–BASS
A Wiley Imprint
www.josseybass.com

Published by Jossey-Bass
A Wiley Imprint
989 Market Street, San Francisco, CA 94103-1741—www.josseybass.com

Jossey-Bass books and products are available through most bookstores. To contact Jossey-Bass directly call our Customer Care Department within the U.S. at 800-956-7739, outside the U.S. at 317-572-3986, or fax 317-572-4002.

Jossey-Bass also publishes its books in a variety of electronic formats. Some content that appears in print may not be available in electronic books.

Library of Congress Cataloging-in-Publication Data

Tulgan, Bruce.
   Not everyone gets a trophy : how to manage generation Y / Bruce Tulgan.— 1st ed.
      p. cm.
   Includes index.
   ISBN 978-0-470-25626-8 (cloth)
   1. Personnel management—United States 2. Generation Y—United States 3. Young adults—Employment—United States 4. Employee motivation—United States I. Title.
   HF5549.2.U5T854 2009
   658.300973—dc22

                                                                                    2008043442

Printed in the United States of America
FIRST EDITION
HB Printing   10 9 8 7 6 5 4 3

● CONTENTS

This book is dedicated to Frances Applegate

NOT EVERYONE GETS A TROPHY

CHAPTER ONE

MEET GENERATION Y
The Most High-Maintenance Workforce in the History of the World

> They keep telling me, "Here's what you get in five years, ten years, twenty years . . ." But they expect me to come back to work tomorrow. What do I get *tomorrow?*
>
> —Gen Yer

Not long ago, the president of a health care consulting firm told me he had just interviewed a twenty-five-year-old man for a job in his firm. The young candidate came to the interview armed with a number of ordinary questions about job duties, salary, and, benefits. When these questions were answered, he made a request: "You should know that surfing is really important to me and there might be days when the surf's really up. Would you mind if I came in a little later on those days?"

••

At a major food conglomerate, summer interns are usually given an assignment, such as a big data-entry project, that they can complete during the course of their summer employment. An executive there shared with me the story of one of his latest interns: "On the first day, she announced she had invented a new cereal. She had a box, complete with artwork and a bag of her cereal inside, that she called her 'prototype.' Clearly she had gone to great lengths, including the recipe and nutritional information and preparing a slide show. She wanted to know when she would be able to pitch her idea to senior executives. 'The sooner the better,' she said."

• •

An experienced nurse-manager in a busy hospital told me she stopped a new young nurse from administering the wrong medicine by intravenous drip to a patient. The manager pulled the young nurse aside and explained emphatically how serious a mistake she almost made. "I explained that this is how patients die unnecessarily. I told her, 'You need to check the wrist bracelet, then the patient's chart, then the charge list, then the IV bag. Then you need to check them *all* again.'" Before she was finished, the young nurse interrupted her. "Actually, you are doing this conversation wrong," she told her boss. "You are supposed to give me some positive feedback before you criticize my work." What did the manager respond? "Okay. Nice shoes. Now, about that IV bag . . ."

• •

A group of executives in the U.S. Peace Corps reported that program administrators receive e-mails on a regular basis from parents making suggestions and requests about the living accommodations and work conditions of their children stationed on missions around the world. One of the Peace Corps executives told me, "I just got an e-mail from a parent saying the meals being provided don't meet his kid's dietary needs. Could we get this young man on a nondairy diet?" The funny thing is that generals in the U.S. Army have told me similar stories about the parents of soldiers.

• •

Another experienced manager, this one in a retail organization, told me an even more striking story. This manager was trying to correct a young associate who had just spoken rudely to a customer. The young man turned to his boss and said, "You know what? I'm thinking about buying this place. And the way you are going, you are going to be the first one out of here!"

• •

Managing people has never been easy. Stuck between employer and employees, managers are tasked with the tough job of negotiating their often competing needs and expectations. But as these stories illustrate, being a manager is even more difficult when a new generation enters the workforce and brings with it new attitudes and behaviors. Every day, leaders and managers in organizations of all shapes and sizes in just about every industry all over the Western world tell me stories about working with the new generation of young employees—the so-called Generation Y—that suggest this might be the most difficult generation to manage yet. Managers tell me:

"They walk in the door on day one with very high expectations."

"They don't want to pay their dues and climb the ladder."

"They walk in the door with seventeen things they want to change about the company."

"They only want to do the best tasks."

"If you don't supervise them closely, they go off in their own direction."

"It's very hard to give them negative feedback without crushing their morale."

"They walk in thinking they know more than they know."

"They think everybody is going to get a trophy in the real world, just like they did growing up."

> Doesn't every new generation of young workers irritate the older, more experienced ones?

It seems to me that the vast majority of leaders and managers think Gen Yers have an attitude problem.

But isn't this always the case when a new generation joins the workforce? Doesn't every new generation of young workers irritate the older, more experienced ones?

At the early career stage of life, young people are just learning to break away from the care of others (parents, teachers, institutions) and taking steps toward self-sufficiency and responsibility. Some do it more slowly than others. As they move into the adult world with the energy and enthusiasm—and lack of experience—that is natural at that stage, they are bound to clash with more mature generations.

And yet as much as human experience—such as the rite of passage into the workforce—stays the same over time, the world doesn't. One epoch may be defined by an ice age, another by global warming. What makes each generation different are these accidents of history that shape the larger world in which human beings move through their developmental life stages. So while every generation rocks the boat when they join the adult world, they also bring with them defining characteristics that alter the rules of the game for everyone going forward.

Gen Yers' "attitude" probably is not likely to go away as they mature; their high-maintenance reputation is all too real. Still, the whole picture is more complicated. Yes, Generation Y will be more difficult to recruit, retain, motivate, and manage than any other new generation to enter the workforce. But this will also be the most high-performing workforce in history for those who know how to manage them properly.

Meet Generation Y

I've been conducting in-depth interviews with young people in the workplace steadily since 1993. That was shortly before the oldest

Gen Yers—those on the cusp of Generation X—started arriving in the workplace as teenagers. Since then, we've followed Gen Yers as they have become the new young workforce and have been developing a comprehensive picture of who they are, how they became that way, and what motivates them. First, to understand the historical context of Generation Y, I'd like to take a few steps back and glance at the accidents of history that defined the generations leading up to Gen Y.

The generation born before the Baby Boom, what I call the Schwarzkopf generation, grew up mostly in the 1930s and 1940s. Their young adulthood was defined by a period of confidence and stability following the upheaval of depression and war. The Baby Boomers, born between 1946 and 1964, were defined by two distinct eras: the first was characterized mostly by the stability of 1950s and early 1960s, while the second coincided with the major social change of the 1960s. Generation X came onto the scene in the 1970s, when adults were steeped in the self-absorption of the "me decade." By the time they came of age in the 1980s and early 1990s, globalization and technology were making the world highly interconnected, rapidly changing, fiercely competitive, and information driven. Their first days at work were also the first days of downsizing—and the last days of job security. While the older workers were hanging on to their desks groaning, "Hold on! It's a workplace revolution! Please, don't downsize me," Gen Xers, in the vanguard of the free-agent mind-set and self-directed career path, shrugged: "Downsize me. Whatever."

Now there is Generation Y.

Although demographers often differ on the exact parameters of each generation, there is a general consensus that Generation X ends with the birth year 1977. Some suggest anyone born between 1978 and 2000 belongs in the Millennial Generation. Given the accelerating pace of change, I think this group is too large. I prefer to break the so-called Millennials into two cohorts: Generation Y (people born between 1978 and 1990) and, for now, Generation Z (anyone born between 1991 and 2000). The oldest among Generation Y are reaching their thirties, but this book is really about the heart of Generation Y, those born during the Reagan years, who grew up mostly in the 1990s, came of age in the 2000s, and are filling up the youth bubble in today's workforce.

Here's the short story with Generation Y. If you liked Generation X, you are going to love Generation Y. Generation Y is like Generation X on-fast-forward-with-self-esteem-on-steroids.

Gen Yers' childhood was defined mostly by the 1990s, and they are reaching their early stage of adulthood amid the profound changes of the 2000s—this era of uncertainty. One could say that the same major historical forces that shaped Generation X are also shaping Generation Y: Globalization and technology, institutions in a state of constant flux, the information tidal wave, and the growing immediacy of everything. But those forces have picked up so much velocity in just one generation that I would argue there is a profound difference in the life experience of Generation Y—a true generational shift.

Globalization and technology have been shaping change since the dawn of time. But during the life span of Generation Y, globalization and technology have undergone a qualitative change. After all, there is only one globe, and it is now totally interconnected. Gen Yers connect with their farthest-flung neighbors in real time regardless of geography through online communities of interest. But as our world shrinks (or flattens), events great and small taking place on the other side of the world (or right next door) can affect our material well-being almost overnight. World institutions—nations, states, cities, neighborhoods, families, corporations, churches, charities, and schools—remain in a state of constant flux just to survive. Authority is questioned routinely. Research is quick and easy. Anyone can get published. We try to filter through the endless tidal wave of information coming at us from an infinite number of sources all day, every day. Nothing remains cutting edge for very long. What we know today may be obsolete by tomorrow. What is beyond belief today may be conventional wisdom by tomorrow. Meanwhile, the pace of everything continues to accelerate. A year is long term, and five years is just a hallucination. Short term is the key to relevance.

In a world defined by constant change, instantaneous response is the only meaningful time frame.

Gen Yers are comfortable in this highly interconnected rapidly changing web of variables. They've never known the world any other way. Uncertainty is their natural habitat. Globalization does not make Gen Yers feel small. Rather, it makes them feel worldly. Technological change does not make them feel as if they are racing to keep up. Rather, it makes them feel connected and powerful. Institutions may be in a state of constant flux, but that's no problem. Gen Yers are just passing through anyway, trying to squeeze out as much experience and as many resources as they can. Authority figures and celebrities may disintegrate for all to see. But this doesn't make Gen Yers cynical. Rather, it gives them faith in everyday heroes. The information tidal wave may inundate us all with more data in one day than anyone could possibly sort through in a lifetime. But this doesn't make Gen Yers feel overwhelmed or uninformed. Rather, it makes them would-be experts on everything. The pace of everything may be accelerating to the point where we expect immediacy in all of our doings. But this doesn't make Gen Yers feel slow. Rather, it makes them impatient. Right now is the only real time. Constant change means you can't count on anything to stay the same. But this doesn't make Gen Yers feel nostalgic. Rather, it makes them feel liberated to abandon what bores them, embrace new things wholeheartedly, and reinvent themselves constantly.

Why are Gen Yers so confident and self-possessed, even in the face of all this uncertainty? One reason is surely that they grew up in the Decade of the Child. Gen Xers were the great unsupervised generation (we made the latchkey into a metaphor). But Generation Y was the great oversupervised generation. In the short time between the childhood of Generation X and that of Generation Y, making children feel great about themselves and building up their self-esteem became the dominant theme in parenting, teaching, and counseling. Throughout their childhood, Gen Yers were told over and over, "Whatever you think, say or do, that's okay. Your feelings are true. Don't worry about how the other kids play. That's their style. You have your style. Their style is valid *and* your style is valid." This is what child psychologists called "positive tolerance," and it was only one small step to the damaging cultural lies that somehow "we are all winners" and "everyone gets a trophy." In fact, as children, most Gen Yers simply showed up and participated—and actually *did* get a trophy.

Every step of the way, Gen Yers' parents have guided, directed, supported, coached, and protected them. Gen Yers have been respected, nurtured, scheduled, measured, discussed, diagnosed, medicated, programmed, accommodated, included, awarded, and rewarded as long as they can remember. Their parents, determined to create a generation of superchildren, perhaps accelerated their childhood. On one hand, kids grow up so fast today (I often say that twelve is the new nineteen); on the other, they seem to stay tightly moored to their parents throughout their twenties. Their early precociousness, in fact, turns into a long-lasting sophomorism. Many psychologists have observed that Gen Yers act like highly precocious late adolescents well into adulthood. (I often say that thirty is the new twenty.)

The power of diversity has finally kicked over the melting pot. Generation Y is the most diverse generation in history in terms of ethnic heritage, geographical origins, ability/disability, age, language, lifestyle preference, sexual orientation, color, size, and every other way of categorizing people. But this doesn't make Gen Yers feel alienated and threatened. Rather, they take the concept of diversity to a whole new level. (I call it *infinite or total diversity*.) To Gen Yers, every single person, with his or her own combination of background, traits, and characteristics, is his or her own unique diversity story. Gen Yers feel little need to conform for the purpose of gaining entry to institutions. For Generation Y, difference is cool. Uniqueness is the centerpiece of identity. Customization of the self is sought after with great zest and originality, through constant experimentation. In the world of Generation Y, the menu of selfhood options is extraordinary and the range of possible combinations infinite.

How do Gen Yers continually shape and reshape their uniqueness? They want to customize anything and everything they possibly can. This goes beyond the services and products they buy. It goes very deep. Gen Yers want to customize their very minds, bodies, and spirits.

Gen Yers customize their minds by customizing their information environment on the Internet. They voraciously pursue an ever-increasing array of mind food—images, sounds, experiences, texts—in an ever increasing range of media and formats, from an ever increasing number of sources, for an ever increasing number of purposes (education, skills training, self-help, health, entertainment, news, household matters, consumer interests, life planning, death planning, spirituality, and so on). They are info junkies compulsively pouring through bits and bytes, mixing and matching the perspectives that appeal to them. Gen Yers know they have more and more information available to them, right at their fingertips, from more and more sources on every conceivable subject. In this environment, Gen Yers have always had the ability to create their own ever-changing personal montage of information, knowledge, and meaning. The ability to access and manipulate information from a wide range of sources gives every individual the opportunity to identify and create meaning with genuine use value and resonance, at least to some online community of interest they can locate or build. In a world with so much perspective, traditional thinking, knowing, and believing are impossible.

They customize their bodies by availing themselves of the wide range of natural and artificial tools and techniques, going way beyond tattoos and piercing and fashion statements. Their efforts range from food obsession to surgery; from Ritalin to naturalism; from yoga to steroids; implants, teeth whitening, tanning cream, and on and on.

Beyond family, they customize their primary relationships across space and time in personalized networks. They even customize spiritual lives of their own devising. Gen Yers often put together bits

> For Generation Y, customization is the holy grail, and it has always been right there within their grasp.

and pieces of the teachings of one or more religious traditions, rejecting others, and ultimately settling on their own selection of values and beliefs and religious or spiritual practices.

For Generation Y, customization is the holy grail, and it has always been right there within their grasp. From the first day, they arrive in the workplace, they are scrambling to keep their options open, leverage their uniqueness for all its potential value, and wrap a customized career around the customized life they are trying to build.

Who Generation Y Is—and Isn't—at Work

Gen Yers don't look at a large, established organization and think, "I wonder where I'll fit in your complex picture." Rather, they look at an employer and think, "I wonder where *you* will fit in *my* life story." Every step of the way, Gen Yers want to find a work situation they can fit into the kind of life they are building for themselves. Because they grew up overly supervised, coached, and constantly rewarded by their parents, Gen Yers will never be content to labor quietly and obediently in a sink-or-swim environment. They are less likely to trust the "system" or the organization to take care of them over time and thus less likely to make immediate sacrifices in exchange for promises of long-term rewards. In fact, the Gen Yer's career path will be a long series of short-term and transactional employment relationships: "What do you want from me? What do you have to offer in return now and for the foreseeable future? I'll stay here as long as it's working out for both of us."

They have very high expectations, first for themselves, but also for their employers. And they have the highest expectations for their immediate bosses. And yet they are more likely to disagree openly with employers' missions, policies, and decisions and challenge employment conditions and established reward systems. They are less obedient to employers' rules and supervisors' instructions. They are less likely to heed organizational chart authority. After all, they had incredibly close relationships with their previous authoritative role models, their parents, who treated them as equals. Instead, Gen Yers respect transactional authority: control of resources, control of rewards, and control of work conditions. Because they look to their immediate supervisors to meet their basic needs and expectations, they freely make demands of them. These are some of the things that Gen Yers tell us in our interviews:

> "My boss keeps telling me, 'This is where you are going to be in five years.' I'm dying to tell him, 'I hate to tell you pal, but you don't know where you're going to be in five years.'"

> "I know they think they are masters of the universe, but, gee, the Soviet Union disappeared overnight. So could they."

> "My boss thinks I have a bad attitude. I don't know why he thinks I have a bad attitude! I told him I'll work alongside him on any project until he drops from exhaustion."

> "They keep telling me, 'This is what you get in five years, ten years, twenty years.' I feel like—what's that expression—they are trying to sell me a bridge."

Precisely because Gen Yers seem to both disregard authority figures and at the same time demand a great deal of them, leaders and managers often find Gen Yers maddening and difficult to manage. Meanwhile, the truth, of course, is more complicated. You see, Generation Y has been much analyzed but, I believe, largely misunderstood. Though in recent years many so-called experts have jumped on the bandwagon of tackling the challenge of "managing Generation Y," nearly everyone I know of is simply reinforcing prevailing misconceptions about Generation Y.

Here are the fourteen most common myths about Generation Y's attitude toward work and career:

Myth #1: Gen Yers are disloyal and unwilling to make real commitments to their employers.

Reality: They can be very loyal. But they don't exhibit the kind of loyalty you find in a kingdom: blind loyalty to hierarchy, tight observance of rites of passage, patience for recognition and rewards. Instead, they offer the kind of loyalty you get in a free market—that is, transactional loyalty (whatever you can negotiate). This is the same kind of loyalty you extend to your customers and clients. We call it "just-in-time loyalty."

••

Myth #2: They won't do the grunt work.

Reality: They are so eager to prove themselves—to you and to themselves—that they will do anything you want them to do. But they won't do the grunt work, or anything else, if they start to fear that nobody is keeping track of what they are doing and giving them credit. They are not about to do the grunt work in exchange for vague, long-term promises of rewards that vest in the deep distant future.

••

Myth #3: They don't know very much and have short attention spans.

Reality: They may not have the same shared knowledge base that people with a certain level of education used to take for granted, but they walk in the door with more information in their heads and more information available at their fingertips than anyone ever has before. They think, learn, and communicate in sync with today's information environment.

••

Myth #4: They want the top job on day one.

Reality: They have no interest in taking their time to "get a feel for the place." They want to hit the ground running on day one. They want to identify problems that nobody else has identified, solve problems that nobody else has solved, make existing things better, invent new things. They want to make an impact.

● ●

Myth #5: They need work to be fun.

Reality: Gen Yers don't want to be humored; they want to be taken seriously. But they do want work to be engaging. They want to learn, to be challenged, and to understand the relationship between their work and the overall mission of the organization. They want to work with good people and have some flexibility in where, when, and how they work.

● ●

Myth #6: They want to be left alone.

Reality: If they actually care one bit about the job, they want managers who know who they are, know what they are doing, are highly engaged with them, provide guidance, help them solve problems, and keep close track of their successes.

● ●

Myth #7: They want their managers to do their work for them.

Reality: They want managers who will spend time teaching them how to do their work very well and very fast.

● ●

Myth #8: They don't care about climbing the proverbial career ladder.

Reality: Gen Yers' career paths will be erratic and eclectic, but that doesn't mean they won't be progressive and developmental. Theirs will be what I call a self-building path made up of learning, relationships, proof of their ability to add value, and lifestyle flexibility. Instead of climbing a ladder, they are making a tapestry.

● ●

Myth #9: Money and traditional benefits don't matter to them.

Reality: Of course, money and benefits matter to them. They want to get the best deal they can get. In fact, they are usually quite savvy about comparing what each employer offers. But money and benefits are only a threshold issue. If you offer money and benefits that are competitive with other comparable employers, then you can keep the conversation going.

•   •

Myth #10: Money is the only thing that matters to them (the opposite of the previous myth, but also widely held by managers who can't believe how brazenly Gen Yers demand money).

Reality: Again, money is a threshold issue. If they are asking for more, what they are really asking is, "What do I need to do to earn more?" Once you meet the threshold of competitive money and benefits, Gen Yers care about five other things: schedule, relationships, task choice, learning opportunities, and location.

•   •

Myth #11: They don't respect their elders.

Reality: They do respect their elders. They are closer to their parents than any other generation has ever been! But they want respect too. Their parents, teachers, and counselors have always treated them with respect, so they feel they deserve respect from their managers, too. Bottom line: they respect what you bring to the table and they want you to respect what they bring to the table.

•   •

Myth #12: They want to learn only from computers.

Reality: From computers, they want to learn stuff that is easy to learn from computers. But, they absolutely need the human element to do their best learning. They learn best from a combination of the human element—coaching, direction, guidance, support, shared wisdom—and the powerful capacity of menu-driven information systems to guide them through the tidal wave of information available at their fingertips.

••

Myth #13: It's impossible to turn them into long-term employees.
Reality: You can turn them into long-term employees. You'll just have to do it one day at a time.

••

Myth #14: They will never make good managers because they are so self-focused.
Reality: Of course, they can be good managers. They just have to learn the basics and then practice, practice, practice.

Bringing Out the Best in Generation Y

The premise of this book is that most of the so-called experts on Generation Y have got it wrong. They argue that since Gen Yers have grown up with self-esteem parenting, teaching, and counseling, the right way to manage them is to praise them and reward them with trophies just for showing up. These "experts" tell managers to create "thank-you" programs, "praise" programs, and "reward" programs. They recommend turning recruiting into one long sales pitch; transforming the workplace into a veritable playground; rearranging training so it revolves around interactive computer gaming; encouraging young workers to find a "best friend" at work; and teaching managers to soft-pedal their authority. In my view, this approach is out of touch with reality.

I tell employers that what Gen Yers need is not always the same as

> Gen Yers' career paths will be erratic and eclectic, but that doesn't mean they won't be progressive and developmental.

> If you want high performance out of this generation, you better commit to high-maintenance management.

what they want. The problem is that giving them what they need successfully is much harder than simply handing them what they want. The high-maintenance Generation Y workforce calls for strong leadership, not weak. Managers should never undermine their authority; should never pretend that the job is going to be more fun than it is; never suggest that a task is within the discretion of a Gen Yer if it isn't; never gloss over details; never let problems slide; and should never offer praise and rewards for performance that is not worthy of them. Instead, managers should spell out the rules of their workplace in vivid detail so Gen Yers can play that job like a video game: if you want A, you have to do B. If you want C, you have do D, and so on.

The rest of this book is meant to help managers and leaders get past the myths about Gen Yers and tackle the issues that make managing them so challenging. In the chapters that follow, I offer nine proven strategies for managing Gen Yers through every step of the employment cycle:

1. Get them on board fast with the right message.

2. Get them up to speed quickly and turn them into knowledge workers.

3. Practice in loco parentis management. Take a strong hand.

4. Give them the gift of context. Help them understand their role in your company and where they fit in *your* picture.

5. Get them to care about great customer service.

6. Teach them how to manage themselves.

7. Teach them how to be managed by you.

8. Retain the best of Generation Y one day at a time.

9. Build the next generation of leaders.

The message of *Not Everyone Gets a Trophy* is simple: if you want high performance out of this generation, you better commit to high-maintenance management. Whether you like it or not, Gen Yers need you to help them form new bonds with your organization, their new roles, new colleagues, and you, their manager. They need you to guide, direct, and support them every step of the way. In return, you'll get the highest-performance workforce in history.

CHAPTER TWO

GET THEM ON BOARD FAST WITH THE RIGHT MESSAGES

Truth in advertising! Don't tell me I'm going to be
making strategy on the beach with beautiful men,
while I sip a glass of wine, connected to the office
remotely—while you give me tons of stock options . . .
unless you are planning to make that happen. Tell
me the real [situation] so I can decide if I want to
be part of your thing.

—*Gen Yer*

Today's talent wars are different from those of the past. Managers today are savvy enough to know that hiring one very good person is better than hiring three or four mediocre people. When the labor pool is tight, that means competing with other employers to attract the very best applicants. The winners in this talent war attract enough candidates that they can be selective in choosing whom to hire. Even so, some managers in a position to be selective still find that when hiring Gen Yers, they often choose the "wrong person." In fact, the most common complaint I hear from managers when it comes to hiring Gen Yers is that they often feel blindsided by a good hire gone bad in the very early stages of employment.

What's going wrong in the hiring of Gen Yers?

Employers eager to attract the best are delivering the wrong messages to the wrong people at the wrong times.

On one end of the labor market, employers are desperate to hire young people for jobs that are not very appealing. That's when employers make the mistake of turning the recruiting process into an elaborate sales pitch. The problem is that prospective employees get the wrong idea about what the job they are applying for is really going to be like. Thus, the new employee is quickly disappointed that the job is not as advertised. In months, sometimes just weeks, the person is unhappy and frustrated. The most common thing we hear from the new young team members is, 'That's not what you told me in the interview.'"

On the other end of the labor market are employers who are very selective in choosing new employees. The problem here is when employers make the hiring process too cumbersome: long delays in the process, wide gaps between a job offer and acceptance and an employee's start date, and lack of communication during those lags.

In order to win today's competition for the most talented young employees, you need to develop a systematic effort to find the right candidates, develop methodical recruiting campaigns anchored in powerful messaging, implement rigorous selection techniques, and then get new staff members in the door on day one excited about the actual experience that awaits them. That is the challenge.

Diversify Your Sourcing

On the high end of the talent spectrum, the demand for highly trained professionals—for example, in health care, high tech, and accounting—is outpacing supply. One understaffed nurse manager told me, "We can't exactly go over to K-Mart and recruit their employees to become nurses, right? We need to compete for the limited pool of people who have made the commitment on their own to get that training." In this situation, employers know exactly where they can find young candidates: among the graduates of lengthy education and certification programs. But competition is fierce among employers seeking the best and the brightest newly minted professionals. The employers on the high end need to set themselves apart so the best young people will want to work for them instead of another comparable organization. To underscore this point, a recent graduate put it best: "I'm at the top of my class, so I have my pick of firms I can work for. So why should I come work for you? You'll have to convince me. I don't want to brag, but I've got a lot of offers already."

On the lower end of the talent spectrum—for example, in retail, hospitality, and cleaning services—employers have the advantage of recruiting among a much wider pool of potential employees. If you are not limited to hiring people who have completed lengthy education and certification programs, then you *can* go over to K-Mart and recruit their employees to come work for you. The problem on this end of the spectrum, employers often tell us, is that the quality and skills of employees in their labor pool are not up to the level they need. One warehouse manager told me, "I don't need to hire rocket scientists, but I need to hire people who show up for work on time and can read and write. Because of geography, the nature of the work we do, and competition from other employers who have more to offer, I can't even hire mediocre performers. I'm scraping the bottom of the barrel here just to get bodies in the door."

Whether you are hiring Gen Yers on the high end or the lower end of the talent spectrum, my guess is that you need to increase your supply of new job applicants. How can you do that?

The first places most managers and organizations go to look for new applicants are the very same places where they've found successful hires in the past. The idea is simple: what's worked for you in the past will probably work for you again. We call this successful-hire profiling. In general, this is a good way to start your talent search. So if you haven't been tracking where your successful hires are coming from thus far, you should start now.

If you are competing for a limited supply of talent, you had better diversify your sources of potential candidates.

But one potential downside of successful-hire profiling is that recruiting from the same sources over and over again can lead to a homogeneous population of employees over time and thus undermine your efforts to develop a diverse workforce. The other potential downside is a bit more obvious: if you are competing for a limited supply of talent, you had better diversify your sources of potential candidates so you can increase your applicant pool.

If step one in a good sourcing process is to look in the same places where you've found successful hires in the past, then step two is to look in places that should be good sources but from which you have not found successful people in the past. If you've sought new employees only from top schools in the past but these sources are not yielding enough applicants now, perhaps it's time to consider looking at top students from second-tier schools. If you've poached talent only from K-Mart in the past, maybe you should consider poaching talent from supermarkets and restaurants. And so on.

What are other ways to widen your pool of candidates?

Friend Referrals

Many employers look to their most successful employees as de facto recruiters. Sometimes this strategy is pursued as part of a company-wide employee-referral program in which employees are encouraged—and even offered incentives—to refer promising job applicants. In other cases, managers simply ask their best employees if they know anyone who might want to join the team. The logic behind formal or informal employee referrals programs is that winners hang out with winners. So what better source of vetted job applicants than the trusted friends of good employees?

Employee referrals are a particularly good way to recruit Gen Yers. Because of their emphasis on personal relationships, Gen Yers are especially interested in bringing their personal connections to their work environment. In fact, human resources departments have been encouraging young employees to have a "best friend at work" in an effort to appeal to Gen Yers' desire for work and life balance. But perhaps more important, helping their friends get a great job makes young employees feel powerful—a feeling they crave.

Rest assured, however, that Gen Yers will not recruit their friends to come work alongside them if they are unhappy in your organization. Sometimes the most successful Gen Yers will do great work for their own personal reasons, even if they are not happy with the job. As one Gen Yer told me about recruiting friends: "They want me to encourage my friends from school to interview here. This place is brutal. Why would I recruit my friends? What kind of friend would I be? I'm just banking as much of their training classes, money, contacts, experience as I can, and then I'm out of here."

If you want Gen Yers to recruit successful new employees among their promising friends and acquaintances, you must ensure they feel good about their job, their boss, and the work experience as a whole. In subsequent chapters, I discuss specific strategies for doing that. If your Gen Yers don't take you up on the chance to recruit their friends, this is worrisome information to which you must pay attention. It is more powerful data than any employee survey can reveal, I promise you.

Assuming that you've successfully encouraged your best, happiest young employees to make referrals, there are several ways to make sure their recommendations result in strong new staff members and a positive experience for the referring employees:

• Make sure referring employees really know your workplace and your expectations as a manager, and have demonstrated consistent good judgment. If you want to make employee referrals a productive source of applicants, you must ensure referring employees understand the hiring criteria with crystal clarity. The essential charge for the referring employee is simple: "Knowing what you know about the company, the position, the hiring manager, and our expectations, do you have good reason to think the referred employee is likely to fit in the organization?"

• Maintain continuous communication with the referring employee every step of the way. You must keep referring employees in the loop when you are communicating with their referred friends or acquaintances. Whether you ask the friend to complete an application, set up an interview, arrange a call-back interview, make an offer, or deliver a rejection, let the referring employee know so he or she is not caught off guard.

• Understand the risks of employee referrals. When Gen Yers go from working with people they consider just colleagues to working with their friends, it often changes the meaning of the job for one or both individuals. Unfortunately, these strong associations may lead to cliques in the workplace and conflict among employees. Also, even if everything goes well with referrals initially, you might make yourself vulnerable to a dual departure risk if something does go wrong.

Although I have observed lots of successful referral sourcing, when I describe the risks of friend-referral sourcing in our seminars, hiring managers sometimes decide the risks outweigh the potential benefits. If you are gun-shy about Gen Y friend-referrals, then what are your other options for diversifying your sourcing?

Finding Gen Yers Online

Of course, Gen Yers are extremely tech savvy, making the Internet an obvious recruiting tool for jobs in any industry and at every skill-level. Most companies already use the Internet to source new talent by finding candidates through data mining, listing positions in online career sites like Monster and industry-specific career networking sites, and attracting prospective employees to their own Web sites. But some employers are trying even more innovative ways to attract young employees. Some are spreading the word about themselves through the blogosphere and social networks or trying to lure Gen Yers through Internet-driven games that draw potential applicants into the company Web site.

If finding candidates through the Internet is a major strategy in your sourcing plan, the most important thing to keep in mind is that your online presence—and particularly your company Web site—better be a good one. This means your Web site should be cutting edge but not clunky or fancy for the sake of being fancy; it should be easy to use with deep menu-driven information systems. If you can lure interested Gen Yers to your internal employment site, it is important to have good streamlining technology in place to narrow the applicant pool. That usually means including a few simple screening questions. Here's the bottom line: if you are not visible and interesting and user-friendly on the Internet, you might as well not exist to Gen Yers.

Tapping Parents, Teachers, and Counselors

So what is the "killer app" when it comes to diversifying your sourcing for promising Gen Y applicants? Funny enough, our research across the board shows that it's a low-tech strategy: seeking referrals from parents, teachers, and counselors. What can you do to tap this source for your organization or yourself as a hiring manager?

Sometimes the most effective referral campaigns are driven by tapping older, more experienced employees for their own children. Who knows the organization better than a more experienced employee? And who knows their children best but parents? The same rules apply to parent-employee referrals as to friend referrals: encourage only satisfied employees with good performance records and evidence of good judgment. Ensure that the hiring criteria are crystal clear. And always keep the lines of communication open with both the referring employee and the referred. One more thing to be aware of is to make sure you don't violate any nepotism rules your company has in place.

Teachers and counselors of Gen Yers are an even better source of referrals because they are more objective. Whether you are hiring employees with high school, college, or graduate degrees, building networks of teachers and counselors who are well respected and dedicated to helping their students is a key strategy when it comes to getting the very best candidates. Of course, you must demonstrate to these teachers and counselors the value proposition of the jobs you offer. And you must convince them that by helping you identify the stars among their students, they too will benefit from a positive reputation among students, parents, their own institutions, and the community of employers for helping students get good jobs.

Deliver a Killer Message

The goal of any recruiting campaign is simple: deliver the most compelling message to large concentrations of potential employees in order to draw a sufficiently large applicant pool so that you can be very selective. You can run the most expensive and extensive recruiting campaign of all time, but if your message is not compelling and believable, you are wasting your time, energy, and money.

Why Your Brand May Not Be Enough to Attract the Best

"We are considered one of the most powerful brands in the world when it comes to consumer markets," said a senior executive in a global beverage company. "That blue chip branding has always carried over to our brand as an employer. Isn't branding a big part of recruiting? Shouldn't that blue chip brand carry some weight with this new generation when they are looking for a job? Isn't that enough to get them in the door?"

The answers are yes, yes, and maybe. Yes, branding is a big part of recruiting. Whether you are a big global brand or a smaller local brand, if Gen Yers know who you are, trust your reputation, and believe you have plenty of resources, often that's enough to get them in the door. But maybe you should hope that branding does not get them all the way in the door. Our research shows that some employers' brands are so famous and "sexy" (think entertainment industry, sports, media) that Gen Yers flock to them—but they do so for the wrong reasons. Gen Yers are attracted by the glamour, excitement, and fantasy attached to the brand, but their unrealistic expectations are often dashed when they discover that what awaits them on the other side of the door is a workplace in which they are expected to do lots of work. This abrupt realization often leads to a disappointing and unsuccessful employment experience.

That's why it's critical to build your brand as an employer, on its own terms, right alongside your brand in the marketplace. Just as your brand in the marketplace is built on the value proposition you offer to consumers, your brand as an employer must be built on the value proposition you offer to employees.

Define Your Value Proposition and Recruiting Message in Gen Yers' Language

Too many employers today are still offering the same long-term career opportunities, together with traditional, old-fashioned rewards they've been offering for decades: slow steps up the organization's ladder, six-month reviews, annual raises, and other standard benefits. "The recruiting message at our firm is crafted by the corporate office with a recruitment advertising firm," one manager in a large consulting firm told me. "The recruiting materials we give interviewees are practically the same ones I got twenty years ago when I started, just prettier. I think some of the senior partners just can't let go of the old 'pay your dues, climb the ladder.' It was always a churn system. Most people get churned out. The tough ones survive and keep moving up. In the long run, you'll get taken care of." If that's your message, then you better wonder why Gen Yers are coming to work for you because it has nothing to do with your message. If all you have to sell are one-size-fits-all career paths and rewards that don't vest until several years in the future, your value proposition and recruiting message will not be compelling to Gen Yers. For this new generation, traditional rewards are merely the threshold test.

What's confusing to many employers, however, is that Gen Yers *appear* very concerned about these long-term opportunities. The executive at the beverage company told me that often Gen Yers are eager to learn about their traditional career track and benefits. She explained, "We have a pretty well-defined career track. Of course, some people go much further or much faster than others, but in general, it's pretty well defined. We describe this track to Gen Yers in the interviews and then again when we make the offers. Usually they'll ask detailed questions about it: What can they expect in five years, ten years, fifteen years? And they seem to understand it all. But eighteen months after taking the job, they walk out the door. When they level with us, they complain they did not get what they wanted fast enough. Why are they asking us these detailed questions in the interviews about five years and ten years and fifteen years?"

So what's going on here? Are Gen Yers just curious? In part, yes. They are curious to know where they'll be in the organization if they were to stay for five, ten, or fifteen years. But this is just-in-case information. Just in case they get stuck in your system, they want to know how that is likely to play out. Another manager asked me, "Are they just humoring us?" Again, the answer is, in part, yes. Gen Yers are savvy enough to know that hiring managers are concerned with retention of new employees and that they should try to express interest in staying for at least some reasonable period of time. What's reasonable? Gen Yers usually assume that whatever time frames you are using to discuss the position must seem reasonable to you, so they mirror that language.

> For this new generation, traditional rewards are merely the threshold test.

A Gen Yer had this to say: "No company says on their Web site, 'Come work for us for a little while, and let's see how it goes.' None of them say in the interviews, 'Well if you work here for six months or a year, it would be fine.' So it would be stupid for me to talk to them like that. I won't say, 'Well, I'm probably only going to stay here for a year until my boyfriend graduates, so hire me.' I mean, who knows? If things are going great for me at the company and it works out for me in terms of my life, then sure, I might stay. So why shouldn't I ask about the long term?"

When it comes to job opportunities, our research shows that Gen Yers look at both the long-term and short-term prospects. They are interested in figuring out what role you might play in their life story, including the long-term possibilities. Since longer term is the language spoken by most employers, asking questions about the long-term opportunities allows Gen Yers to compare employers more easily. Often when Gen Yers ask questions about short-term opportunities, employers have a hard time speaking that language. And sometimes Gen Yers find that asking those questions turns off potential employers and leaves the Gen Yer without a job offer. They don't usually make that mistake twice.

Still, what really concerns Gen Yers are the short-term opportunities and rewards. If you want to speak to them in a way that separates your job offer from the others right now, you have to talk about right now. You have to talk about what you have to offer them today, tomorrow, next week, this month, the first six months, and the first year. If you want your recruiting message to attract them, then you need a recruiting message that speaks to their real concerns.

Of course, every applicant is unique and comes with his or her own concerns to the table. They want different things from different jobs at different times. In our research, we've learned that what work means to Gen Yers at any given time changes depending on what's going on in their lives. Sometimes they want to hide out and collect a paycheck. I call this a *safe harbor job*. There are no upsides for the employer. Don't let anyone in the door who expects to hide out and collect a paycheck. Sometimes Gen Yers are taking stock and trying to figure out what they really want to do next. I call this a *weigh station job*. The one potential upside here for the employer is that the Gen Yer may well try to build a record of accomplishment working for you so he or she will be able to trade that success for the job he or she really wants.

Sometimes they look at work as a place to hang out with friends. I call this a *peer group job*. The potential upside for the employer is that Gen Yers may really look forward to coming to work. The downside is that their social relations will be their primary focus. Sometimes Gen Yers find work that aligns with their deep interests and priorities. I call this a *passion job*. The upside for the employers is that they will bring energy and enthusiasm to the work. The potential downside arises when the work part of work makes the passion seem more like a grind.

Sometimes Gen Yers see a job as an opportunity to work like crazy for a period of time with the chance of a giant payoff. I call this a *big gamble job*. The upside is that they will work like crazy. The downside is that if they lose confidence in the likelihood of the giant payoff, they might "strip-mine" the organization for any resources they can find—training opportunities, business contacts, paper clips—to try to give themselves a return on what starts to look like a bad investment.

Sometimes what Gen Yers value in a job is an unusual opportunity to meet an idiosyncratic need or want. It might be to work a very particular schedule, or work with particular individuals, or work in a particular location, or learn a particular skill, or do a particular task, or engage in some nonwork activity (sleeping or reading or watching television) on the job. I call this a *needle-in-a-haystack job*. The upside is that as long as they value that needle in a haystack need or want and you are able to provide it, they won't leave.

The best case is when Gen Yers are looking at the job as a chance to make an impact while building themselves up with your resources. They hope to learn, grow, and collect proof of their ability to add value. I call this a *self-building job*. As long as you keep supporting their self-building, this will bring out their best for the most sustained period.

The trick for hiring managers and organizations is creating a recruiting message that will attract employees who are looking for a self-building job. There are eight self-building factors Gen Yers look for in employment opportunities:

1. *Performance-based compensation.* Financial compensation must be competitive in the marketplace. But much more important than the actual salary, Gen Yers want to know that their compensation is not limited by any factor other than their own performance. They want to be assured that if they work harder and better, they will be rewarded in direct proportion to the value they add.

2. *Flexible schedules.* Gen Yers want to know that as long as they are meeting goals and deadlines, they will have some control over their own schedules. The more control, the better.

3. *Flexible location.* Again, as long as they are meeting goals and deadlines, Gen Yers want to know that they will have some control over where they work. To the extent that working in a particular space in a particular building is required, they want to know that they will have some power to define their own space (arrange furniture, computers, art work, lighting) to their liking.

4. *Marketable skills.* Gen Yers are looking for formal and informal training opportunities and want to be assured that they will be building skills and knowledge faster than they would become obsolete.

5. *Access to decision makers.* Gen Yers don't want to wait until they climb the ladder to build relationships with important leaders, managers, clients, customers, vendors, or coworkers. They want access right away.

6. *Personal credit for results achieved.* Gen Yers don't want to work hard to make somebody else look good. They want to put their own names on the tangible results they produce.

7. A *clear area of responsibility.* Gen Yers want to know that they will have 100 percent control of something, anything, so they can use that area of responsibility as their personal proving ground.

8. *The chance for creative expression.* Gen Yers want to have a clear picture of the parameters that will constrain their creativity so they can imagine the terrain in which they will have freedom to do things their own way.

This, in a nutshell, is what Gen Yers want. And they expect these things sooner rather than later. If you can offer Gen Yers the chance to build themselves up—in the short run—using your resources, then you will have a compelling message.

But don't try to sell Gen Yers a bill of goods. Don't promise them these things if you can't offer them. Overselling the job to Gen Yers is a big mistake. If you sell them a self-building opportunity falsely, they will quickly turn the job into a safe harbor or a way station or a peer group experience.

Instead, clarify expectations at the outset by answering the fundamental questions that are really on their minds: "Exactly what will you expect me to do today, tomorrow, next week, this month, next month, and the month after that? And exactly what do you have to offer me in the form of financial and nonfinancial rewards today, tomorrow, next week, this month, next month, and the month after that?"

Answer those questions in terms that speak to Gen Yers' real concerns right now. Tell it like it is.

Be Very Selective

The point of crafting a compelling recruiting message is to attract a sufficiently large applicant pool from which you can choose selectively. The biggest mistake hiring managers make is continuing the "attraction campaign" until the job candidate has accepted the job and sometimes until the new employee is already at work. We call this "selling candidates all the way in the door." Why is this a problem? Because in an effort to sell, sell, sell their job to a candidate, sometimes companies make promises they can't keep—or sell the job to the wrong candidate.

The result of selling candidates all the way in the door is often that many new employees quickly begin to experience a form of buyer's remorse: "This job is not what they sold me!" They may be disappointed and unhappy and yet remain in the job, sometimes for months on end. And this is the number one cause of early voluntary departures for Gen Yers. One Gen Yer described her situation:

"The whole interview process was a sell job. The whole time they kept asking me if I had questions for them. So I asked a lot of questions, and they gave me a lot of answers, but I realize now they were just telling me what they thought I wanted to hear, and I bought it totally. The job is not at all what they told me it was going to be."

In a tight labor market, the pressure to hire also leads to hard-selling a job to a candidate, even if that person is not ideal for the job. In fact, so many employers are so starved for young talent that they just can't bear to turn potential employees away, even in the face of huge red flags telling them, "DON'T HIRE THIS PERSON!" An executive in e-business and technology told me, "We've had candidates come late for their interviews or even miss interviews, and then we hire them anyway because they look good on paper. Sometimes people will interview badly, someone will get a bad feeling, but the rest of us will talk that person into going ahead with hiring because we are just scrambling."

The first rule of selection is: *It is better to leave a position unfilled than to fill it with the wrong person*. When job candidates display failings in the job selection process that would make them bad employees, these are red flags. Pay attention to red flags! They don't have to disqualify an applicant, but they should shift your presumption away from hiring the person. You should require a lot of hard evidence to overcome red flags.

The second rule of selection is: *Remember, you are not the only one selecting. The employee is selecting you too*. Even after you've sold the job and the organization to a candidate with your recruiting message, the selection process is the key to closing the deal for both of you. No matter how much you may decide you want the person, if you don't make the selection process fast, you will lose a lot of very good potential Gen Y employees. The hard part is that in addition to being fast, you must be rigorous. There are several ways to make your selection process fast and rigorous.

Scare Them Away

Eliminate the Gen Y job candidates who only think they are serious. How? After you are done selling Gen Yers up to the door, try to

> Eliminate the Gen Y job candidates who only think they are serious.

scare them away. Tell them all the downsides of the job in clear and honest terms. What does that look like? Tell people, "Come work for us, and you will be expected to do more work and better work than you've ever done before. We'll keep pushing you to work longer, smarter, and faster all day, every day." See who is left. Think about the U.S. Marine Corps recruiter who reminds the would-be Marine before he signs on the dotted line, "You realize that the thirteen-week boot camp is very tough? You'll be doing push-ups in the mud at 4:00 A.M.? Then eventually we are probably going to send you abroad into harm's way. And by the way, we don't pay very much." You should do the same, whatever your job. If you run a warehouse, make it clear that your new young employees will carry a lot of heavy boxes. If you run an accounting firm, make it clear that your new young accountants will do a lot of repetitive document handling and put in lots of long hours. And so on.

Testing

Whoever is left after you've tried to scare them away is worth testing. In our seminars for hiring managers, we recommend testing serious job applicants to further verify their seriousness and get a quick baseline reading of their aptitude in key areas of the job for which you are considering them. Some employers believe strongly in personality tests and general aptitude tests. My own view is that even if you are using research-validated tests, the results can often be confusing to the employee and the employer. If you use these tests, make sure someone on your recruiting team knows how to really interpret them. Sometimes a trusted outside expert is your best bet.

Whatever testing method you use, try to devise a fast and penetrating test that goes quickly to the heart of the basic tasks and responsibilities the person will be expected to do if hired. If you are hiring people to do data entry, ask them to enter a bunch of data. If you are hiring people to stack boxes, ask them to stack a bunch of boxes. This doesn't mean that applicants have to know every-thing—or anything, for that matter—about how to do the job before they are hired. Simply asking several applicants to complete the same job-related test will give you a good idea of where they stand in relation to each other. An experienced carpenter in charge of a large crew told me, "Whenever I'm hiring a carpenter's helper, I'll have him move a stack of long boards from one place to another. I just want to see how he handles that. Does he know how to walk straight so he doesn't swing the boards around and smack into something or someone? How fast can he move them? This one little test tells me a lot, even about someone who has never been on a construction site. Some people have a natural sense about them physically, and some people don't. If you don't, you're probably not going to be very successful as a carpenter's helper. But if you can do that pretty well, then I'll sit down and talk to you."

Another approach is to ask applicants to submit a proposal out-lining exactly how they intend to add value in the organization. Give them no further guidance if you want to test their resource-fulness and their creativity and ability to operate in a sink-or-swim environment. On the other hand, if you want to see how well appli-cants are able to follow detailed instructions, you might give them this same assignment, but with detailed guidelines for how to com-plete the proposal.

Whatever test you settle on, just make sure you can implement and evaluate it with relative speed. And make sure you know in advance exactly what you are looking for. What are you testing for? Skill? Ability? Will? Work habits? Intangibles like attitude and diligence?

The Behavioral Job Interview

Then comes the job interview, the one employment selection process almost every manager does, but very few do well. Some orga-nizations impose meticulous control over the job interview process.

Usually these organizations have the best interviews because they have worked hard to develop a thorough behavioral interviewing process. Often they are smart enough to require any manager who interviews job candidates to receive training in how to conduct interviews properly. Unfortunately, such organizations are the exception. In most organizations, hiring managers have a huge amount of latitude when it comes to conducting job interviews.

Gen Yers tell us horror stories every day about job interviews. Interviewers sometimes ask inappropriate questions like, "What was it like growing up in your family?" Or, "Do you intend to have children?" Sometimes they ask irrelevant and silly questions such as, "What can you do in the next sixty seconds that will really impress me?" But a surprising number of interviewers simply go through an applicant's résumé out loud, reading it often for the first time, asking for amplification here and clarification there. Many just want to "get to know the applicant" by chatting informally about sports or clothes or classes the applicant took in college. Some blowhard interviewers explicitly waste the interview by doing all the talking themselves instead of hearing from the applicants. These approaches leave interviewers with little to evaluate other than whether they got a "good impression" of the interviewee. That's because too often managers who are conducting interviews have no method to their interviewing.

When it comes to interviewing, the best practice is behavioral interviewing. Although there are entire courses taught in behavioral interviewing, I often teach it to managers in my seminars in three minutes. Behavioral interviewing simply means asking applicants to tell you a story and then listening to their story: "Tell me a story about a time you solved a problem at work." Or, "Tell me a story about a conflict you had with another employee at work. How did you solve it?"

If you want to take behavioral interviewing to the next level, here's a simple list of questions in two main areas—performance and skills—we've developed to help managers conduct behavioral interviewing:

Performance

- Please tell me about a specific instance when you . . .
  - Identified a specific type of problem
  - Solved a specific type of problem
  - Accomplished a particular task
  - Were charged with a particular kind of responsibility
  - Worked in a particular type of situation
  - Worked in a particular set of conditions
- What was successful about your approach?
- What was unsuccessful about your approach?
- What did you learn?
- What would you do differently?
- If you worked for us, you would have to do X. How would you approach the challenge?

Skill

- Please tell me about a specific instance when you used [fill in the appropriate skill].
- What was successful about your approach?
- What was unsuccessful about your approach?
- What did you learn?
- What would you do differently?
- What ancillary skills were useful to you?
- How have you developed this skill further since then?
- In the specific instance you described, what related skill did you use other than the skill I asked about?
- If you worked for us, you would have to use [fill in the appropriate skill]. How would you approach the challenge?

The Realistic Job Preview

When the Gen Yer you hire finally walks in your front door for the first day of work, I promise you she has a particular idea in her head of what that job is going to be like. That idea may have come from the research she has done on the Web. Or it may have come from the sales pitch she got in the recruiting process, or from her own fantasies about what she hopes the job will be like. The question is: Does that idea bear any resemblance to the real job she is going to face?

One mistake a lot of organizations make is that although they provide prospective employees with job previews, they are not realistic previews. And this goes way beyond the recruiting literature. Often employers create elaborate internship programs in order to develop prospective new employees. This is especially common in professional services firms, but is also a practice used widely by organizations that devote any substantial resources to recruiting young talent through teachers, professors, or career counselors in schools (as you should). The problem is that internship programs are often seen as part of the recruiting campaign and not a meaningful part of the selection process. As such, many of these programs are set up to lavish especially interesting assignments on young interns and offer exposure to important decision makers, learning opportunities, and fun outings. As many associates in law firms will tell you, summer associates are often referred to by the full-time associates as "summer partners" because they are so well treated. One senior associate in a major New York City law firm said, "No wonder they are a little taken aback when they finally finish taking the bar exam and show up for work after Labor Day. We load tons of work on them and tell them they are expected to bill two thousand hours a year, and they want to know, 'When do we get to go to the baseball game like we did when I was here last summer?'"

If your job descriptions and job posting all read like sales literature or if your internships are part of the recruiting sales process, then you need to include a realistic job preview as part of the selection process. Otherwise the new employee's first day of work is going to be the first real preview of what the job actually looks like. And that's too late. There are few things Gen Yers are more sensitive to than false advertising. They will spread the word if they feel duped. If you don't create a realistic job preview for them in advance, they may create a hyperrealistic or totally unrealistic but very negative preview of your company for the world.

> There are few things Gen Yers are more sensitive to than false advertising. They will spread the word if they feel duped.

There are many ways to provide accurate job previews, including these:

- A probationary hiring period. This can be a few weeks in which you can try out the employee and the employee can try out the job for a while.
- A realistic internship. Make sure to assign them real tasks that mirror the actual tasks, responsibilities, and projects they will be asked to do if they accept the job. Make sure to include the grunt work.
- A "job shadow" or "tag along" with another person in your organization who is doing the same job this person will be doing if hired. This approach is sometimes used in hospitals. Make sure the would-be health care workers get to see sick patients, bedpans being emptied, and some of the other tough tasks they'll have to handle. By tagging along for several days, a week or more, your applicant will get a good picture of what the job entails. You will also get the double bonus of having the existing employee who is shadowed spend a lot of time with the applicant in the job setting. This often leads to existing employees coming in and saying, "Hey, I hope we are going to hire this person!" Or, "Hey, we are not going to hire this person, are we?" Their feedback will tell you a lot. If applicants can't job-shadow, perhaps you can give them an opportunity to watch people doing the actual job. Sometimes on factory floors or in restaurant kitchens, the best thing you can do is let a prospective employee watch people work on the line for a while. If even that's

not possible, produce a video of people in your organization performing the key tasks and responsibilities of the job, and provide an opportunity for the candidate to review the video.

- Create a print document that is the opposite of a recruiting brochure. Instead of trying to sell the job, explain exactly how a person with this job will spend his day moment by moment.

- Sometimes the best thing you can do to create a realistic job preview is encourage your employees to engage in very frank discussions with applicants in which they are not trying to sell the job but are actively trying to give a clear picture of what the job really is like.

Close the Deal Fast

Sometimes employers do a good job attracting qualified Gen Yers into their applicant pool, but then create huge delays in the selection process. So please allow me to offer—one more time—the caveat I have made throughout the preceding section. As important as it is to be very selective in your hiring of Gen Yers, you also *must do it fast*. If you move too slowly, you will lose a lot of great hiring prospects. The two watchwords of your selection process should be *rigorous* and *fast*.

Even if you succeed in expediting your selection process, make a solid offer, and get an unconditional acceptance, your prospect is still not safely on board. Offer and acceptance, to Gen Yers, does not always an iron-clad deal make. Sometimes Gen Yers just change their minds. Sometimes they get cold feet. Perhaps a better offer comes their way. Or it may not be another job offer. Take, for example, this Gen Yer's story: "I had accepted an offer, set a start date that was two months down the road, and even took an advance on my pay. But some of my friends were going on this amazing trip to Latin America, and I just couldn't say no to them. When I tried to change my start date by six weeks, the company told me I couldn't. So I told them forget it. I returned the advance, and I got a great job when I got back."

But more often, Gen Yers lose the interest generated during the highly engaged communication that usually characterizes the attraction and selection process. I realize that sometimes there is an unavoidable time lag between the time an offer of employment is made and accepted and day one of the actual job. Maybe the employee needs to finish school, or the employer must complete a security screening. Whenever possible, avoid these delays because they are minefields of vulnerability in which a perfectly good hiring can go bad.

If such a delay is unavoidable, here are a few ways to keep newly hired Gen Yers engaged and excited about joining your company:

- Maintain a high level of communication during the intervening time. Stay in touch by scheduling a series of interesting, engaging, useful communications—not just from human resources or some other anonymous corporate office, but rather from the hiring manager and the team the employee will be working with.

- Send them plenty of background material on the company, but also include polo shirts, caps, magnets, mugs, pens, and other paraphernalia that will help her show off their new job to their friends and acquaintances.

- Send actual assignments (not too time-consuming) for them to complete and return. These should not be pro forma assignments, but assignments that will help new employees jump-start the orientation process when they arrive. Are there any ongoing matters in which you could include them? Could you include them in team memos? Could you invite them (but not require them) to attend team meetings? What forms will they have to fill out when they arrive? Are there personnel lists you can provide? Is there a facebook so they can start to familiarize themselves with key people up the chain of command and key people on their team?

- Consider having key people on the team send e-mails or actual letters introducing themselves and explaining where they fit on the team and what, if any, working relationship they are likely to share.

All of these communication options have the effect of staying in touch with your newly hired employees. It makes them feel that they are actively transitioning to the work: they are accepted by their new workplace and being integrated into the team. It also gives them a tiny bit of a realistic job preview. Whatever you do, avoid radio silence during the intervening time between the offer and acceptance and day one.

Meanwhile, never forget that day one is going to be the most important day for this new employee, so prepare for it as if the success of the hire depends on it—because it might.

CHAPTER THREE

GET THEM UP TO SPEED QUICKLY AND TURN THEM INTO KNOWLEDGE WORKERS

I was so psyched on my first day. I came crashing through door like, "I'm here!" They were like, "Oh right, we forgot you were starting today." The guy who hired me was looking at me like I was from another planet. He had me sit in a conference room, fill out a bunch of forms, and look through some binders. They kept me in that conference room for three weeks. Every time I'd beg a manager, "Put me in, coach" they would respond, "Just sit tight. We're not quite ready for you yet." They kept telling me, "Relax, we're paying you. It's our time now." That's where they were wrong. That was *my* time. They were wasting *my* time.

—*Gen Yer*

In our research, we often hear about this day-one disconnection between new Gen Y employees and their bosses. Gen Yers tell us about arriving for work excited and enthusiastic about the new challenges ahead, only to find that their feelings are not completely requited by the managers who await them in the workplace. For their part, managers often find Gen Yers' day-one enthusiasm to be inconvenient at best, and sometimes downright off-putting.

A senior manager in a financial services firm told me, "They show up like they expect the top job on their first day. That's *my* job. I know you are excited that this is your first day of work, so I hate to tell you, kid, that for me, this is just another Monday. So go fill out these documents for HR, then look around for work. Sometimes I'll tell the new analysts, 'Just start moving your arms and legs, and pretty soon you'll be doing what everybody else is doing.'" This manager explained that his firm brings in an "incoming class" of about twenty-five new analysts, mostly brand-new college graduates, each year, but only about half of them make it past the first six months. Gee, I wonder why.

We've learned that hit or miss is more the rule than the exception when it comes to getting Gen Yers up to speed in today's workplace. Maybe you could get away with that in the workplace of the past with the workforce of the past, but Gen Yers won't let you get away with it. This is what a Gen Yer told me about her experience: "Probably ten different people told me I was too enthusiastic in my first three months here. 'Your enthusiasm makes you seem immature,' is what one very experienced manager told me. 'Nobody takes you seriously until you've been here for three years anyway.' Three years?! You think I'm going to wait around this place for three years until somebody takes me seriously! Not a chance. If I'm not taken seriously here, then you can be sure I won't be working here in three years."

Gen Yers want to hit the ground running on day one. But they don't want to be thrust into sink-or-swim situations either. They want to hit the ground running with lots of support and guidance every step of the way. It may be exhausting for managers, but if you don't plug into their excitement and enthusiasm on their way in the door, you are in serious danger of turning a good hire bad.

> Gen Yers want to hit the ground running on day one.

Gen Yers almost always walk in the door with a spark of excitement. The question is, Do you pour water or gasoline on that spark? Here's how you pour gasoline on the spark: grab hold of them on their way in the door (*grab* is a metaphor, of course) and don't let them go.

Grab Hold of Them, and Don't Let Them Go

We have a simple rule we teach managers in our seminars: day one is the most important day. You have to plan for Gen Yers' first day of work like you plan for your kid's birthday party. That doesn't mean you greet them with candles and balloons and gifts and song. But you do have to greet them.

Consider the greetings the U.S. Marine Corps offer to brand-new Gen Y recruits. The Marines have a well-known onboarding program called boot camp. For thirteen solid weeks, they provide an all-encompassing 24/7 experience in which they take an ordinary human being and transform that person into a Marine—a person with a unique set of values and a unique set of skills, a person so connected to the Marine Corps and its mission and every other Marine that this person is now ready to walk into the line of fire, literally, and win battles. Now that's what I call a greeting.

The Marines don't pay much. Their job is hard and dangerous. Yet they are able to build forty thousand new Marines every year with a washout rate that is so low it can hardly be measured. Learn a lesson from the most effective employer of eighteen to twenty-two year olds in the Western world. When you are thinking about shaping your orientation process for Gen Yers, think about how you can emulate the boot camp approach.

You don't need obstacle courses and firing ranges. And you don't need to make your newly hired employees do push-ups in the mud at 4:00 A.M. What matters is replicating the intensity, the connection to mission, the feeling of shared experience and belonging to a group, the steady learning, and the constant challenge. It's about taking Gen Yers seriously on day one and every other day.

In one consulting firm I know with about a hundred employees and very limited training resources, here's what they do with the four or five Gen Yers they hire each year. From the moment an applicant accepts an offer of employment, that person is assigned to three experienced employees, called advisers, who work with the new employees from day one. Between the day an applicant accepts the job offer and the new employee's first day at the company, the advisers take turns staying in touch with that person, are involved in setting his start date, and are expected to take responsibility for orientation and initial training. "The advisers stick to the new staff like glue," the CEO of this firm told me. "Our goal is simple. The new staff should never be alone for one minute in the first six months if the advisers can possibly help it."

The mistake employers often make is investing time, energy, and money in a highly engaging orientation program for Gen Yers and immediately afterward depositing them into a demoralizing no-support workplace. Following the intensity of the orientation program, Gen Yers end up being greeted in the real workplace by coworkers and managers with the same, "We forgot you were coming," "Cool your jets," and "Start moving your arms and legs" messages. No matter how long and intense (or how short and mundane) your orientation process is, you cannot ever let Gen Yers alone to sink or swim. The longer you sustain the intensity and support, the more value you will get out of your Gen Y employees. The consulting firm CEO told me: "There are supposed to be three advisers, but usually one of the advisers will really own a new staff person and carry a disproportionate amount of the weight. But they are the smart ones because this is a small organization, and it gives them their own power base. They have these die-hard dedicated protégés who always want to work on their projects and these protégés break their backs for their advisers."

Low Tech: Train Them One Task at a Time

Gen Yers, especially the best and brightest, are eager to hit the ground running and take on more and more challenges and responsibility. This is what a Gen Yer recently told me: "You want me to be really into this job, right? You want me to love it? Then make it lovable. I'm not going to be all fired up about doing the same thing day after day. Give me a challenge. Give me a chance to do something bigger and better. I'm willing to work my ass off. But give me something I can be fired up about."

This kind of enthusiasm and desire to take on challenges is extremely valuable, but it also puts a huge amount of pressure on Gen Yers' immediate supervisors. A senior manager in the buying organization of a large retail chain shared this experience: "One of my direct reports always tells me, 'I've done that before,' as if that is a good reason for me to give her a different assignment. 'I am giving you this assignment *because* you know how to do it,' I say. But I know what she really means is that she is not feeling challenged. She'll work more than most of the people around here. If I am going to take advantage of her willingness to take on these new challenges, I have to find the time to teach her. I can't just give her a new challenge and say, 'Go for it.'"

Gen Yers, especially the most capable and ambitious among them, push hard for more significant roles with increased responsibilities at much earlier stages in their careers than new young workers of generations past. It's not just misplaced arrogance on their part, but rather a result of their natural adaptation to the information environment. The nature of professional learning today is a continuous just-in-time all-the-time endeavor. Gen Yers have never known it any other way. That's why they are always in a hurry to advance to the next skill set or the next task, responsibility, or project—even when they seem clearly not ready from your perspective.

Listen to one engineering group leader in a nuclear weapons research laboratory: "They want to step into bigger roles much sooner than they are ready. They look at me playing this role and they think 'Yeah, I could do that.' But they don't realize how much there is to this role, how many different responsibilities are involved, and what expertise and experience are necessary to handle all those responsibilities." From the standpoint of many managers, of course, each new task, responsibility, and project Gen Yers want to take on looks like a huge bundle of best practices and standard operating procedures to learn, pitfalls to avoid, resources to command, and judgment calls to be made. Managers tell me all the time, "In our line of work, it's especially challenging to give inexperienced young people significant responsibilities. Perhaps a new young person could learn the knowledge and skill necessary to do one of these tasks and responsibilities, or two, or three, or four. But the role they want is too complex to hand over in its entirety to someone without several years of experience." I promise you, I've been told that by leaders in supermarkets and nuclear weapons labs alike—and everybody in between. We call this the "meaningful roles problem."

The simple fact is that if it takes you months or years to get Gen Yers up to speed and into meaningful roles on your team, then you'll have serious problems keeping high-potential Gen Yers engaged and growing. Don't tell me you are struggling to manage and retain the best Gen Yers and then tell me it's going to take months or years before they can do important work that allows their coworkers and bosses to take them seriously.

How can you handle this conundrum? You may have to unbundle complex roles and then rebuild them one tiny piece at a time. You can give Gen Yers meaningful work at early stages in their tenure if you commit to teaching and transferring to them one small task or responsibility at a time.

Here is a great example that the same engineering group leader from that nuclear weapons research laboratory shared with me: "I learned from the mechanics here who are short-staffed. They teach new mechanics to do one simple task very well. Then after the new mechanics do that task for a few days, they add another simple task, and so on. After a few weeks, the new mechanics have a dozen things they can do pretty well, and they are full-fledged members of the team, but with a much smaller repertoire. The really ambitious ones keep adding one task after another and build pretty big repertoires within a few months. So I decided to do that with my new project engineers. I give them one tiny little piece of the project. I'll sit with them and teach, then let them have a tiny little piece of work. When they get that tiny little piece of work done, I'll teach them another piece. And another. It is very effective with the new young engineers. They actually like it this way. They are doing less, but they feel like they are doing more."

> Remember that Gen Yers want to learn from people, not just from computers.

It may be very high-tech work they are doing in that nuclear weapons lab, but this is low-tech training at its best. Remember that Gen Yers want to learn from people, not just from computers. If you are willing to be the teacher, you can support Gen Yers in their desire to acquire the ability to learn new things very quickly. You can train them the old-fashioned way in short-term stages that track directly with adjustments in their day-to-day responsibilities. Every new task turns into a proving ground, which enables them to demonstrate proficiency and earn more responsibility right away. I realize this approach to training Gen Yers requires a high degree of engagement and ongoing teaching and managing. But that's how you can keep Gen Yers growing fast over the first, and the second, and the third year. Who knows? You might even be able to help them gain depth and wisdom way beyond their years.

High Tech: Don't Fight Their Desire for the Latest and Greatest Information Technology

So often I go into an organization that is trying to retool its training practices to suit what they think Gen Yers want and need. "The latest and greatest technology," said one training leader in a major international consumer products company. "We are making all the ongoing training just-in-time. Everything is going to be a computer game."

Here's the good news: you do not have to turn everything (or anything really) into a computer game to plug into Gen Yers' learning needs. But you really should make the effort to get them the technology they are so comfortable and adept at using.

There is so much information produced in a day in any area of expertise that Gen Yers' default presumption is that nobody could possibly learn all that information, even after studying for one hundred years. Given the pace of change, information becomes obsolete so fast that it seems less important how much you know or have known, and more important how quickly you can learn new things and put them into action. As one Gen Yer put it: "Gotta keep learning. Gotta keep moving. All the stuff you've forgotten, I'll never have to know. Half the stuff you remember, I'll never have to know. That just means I'm way past halfway to catching up to you. It's the obsolescence curve getting steeper and steeper. It makes it a whole lot easier for a guy my age to catch up to the more experienced people."

Yes, Gen Yers want the latest and greatest technology. But it's not just a desire for the coolest toy. It's like breathing. It's their connection to the larger information environment. For Gen Yers, the information technology imperatives are simple:

- Constant connectivity with whomever they want
- Immediate access to whatever information they want
- Total customization of their information environment
- The ability to learn from and collaborate with experts in real time

Gen Yers have high expectations that their employers will provide them with the latest and greatest technology, and they complain bitterly when they don't get the tools they expect.

What Gen Yers want from technology-based learning is not depth and wisdom, but rather to fill skill and knowledge gaps that slow them down in their daily work. One Gen Yer told me, "I laid out some cash of my own to get the handheld I need to be effective. I have tried to get reimbursed, and I'll keep trying. But the thing is, I can do my job so much better and so much easier with the hardware I got myself that it's worth it even if they never pay up."

They know what's out there, and they want to be able to use it. Gen Yers want to learn what they need to learn when they need to learn it, not because they are lazy and not because they have short attention spans. To them, Web-based search technology, online resources, social networking, and wiki tools are everyday tools like the telephone. When you tell them that they won't have access to those tools to fill skill and knowledge gaps all day long, it's like you are telling them to work in the Stone Age. Imagine if someone told you in the early 1990s that you would have to use carbon paper to keep copies of your documents. That's what it sounds like when you tell Gen Yers you don't want them to use the tools available to them.

Here's a story I was told by several people at a large insurance company. It seems that a young hotshot Gen Yer in the marketing department (I'll call him Barry) had been given a temporary assignment for several months—and a BlackBerry to use during this assignment. But when the temporary assignment ended, Barry was asked to turn in his BlackBerry. Hoping that the whole thing would be forgotten in such a large company and that he would be left with his treasured BlackBerry, Barry ignored those requests. Not long after, Barry found himself in a meeting with his boss and several senior managers (all of them armed with BlackBerrys because of their senior positions). At some point, an important question came up before the group that fell into the purview of Barry's boss, who demurred, saying he would have to look up the answer after the meeting and get back to everybody. Meanwhile, Barry began researching the question in earnest, tapping away on his BlackBerry. Before the meeting ended, Barry raised his hand and offered a detailed answer to the important question that had been put to his boss. As one person in attendance at the meeting said, "We were all very impressed. Suffice to say, we decided that Barry could keep that BlackBerry."

This is the Gen Yers' information environment. With search engines and menu-driven information systems, anyone can find multiple answers from multiple sources to answer any question in a heartbeat. Shared work

> To Gen Yers, Web-based search technology, online resources, social networking, and wiki tools are everyday tools.

product libraries take typical search technology to a whole new level by providing instant quality vetting. With access to a shared work product library, employees can avoid reinventing the wheel by accessing past high-quality work product, which can be tapped for quick learning as well as lifted and reused to jump-start similar projects. Wiki technology is the ultimate collaboration facilitator by enabling different individuals to contribute to a work product from remote locations on their own time. Social networking allows anyone to build mutually rewarding relationships with people of similar interests—inside the company or outside—regardless of geography or other boundaries. Instant messaging means anyone can ask anyone they "know" anything at any time. Imagine a mind-set in which these tools—and the corresponding connectivity, immediacy, constant access, and total customization—are taken for granted. The only question is, What are you doing to facilitate Gen Yers' use of these tools to increase their effectiveness at work?

Put the tools in their hands, and watch them fill one tiny information gap at a time in real time. This is the high-tech analogue to learning one task at a time. With access to the technology they know and love, Gen Yers will fine-tune and nuance their on-the-job learning in ways that might shock and delight you.

Turn Every Employee into a Knowledge Worker

Especially when they are new on the job, Gen Yers are eager to identify problems that nobody else has identified and solve problems that nobody else has solved. They want to improve what's already there, and they want to invent new things. One Gen Yer told me, "Before I even started my job, I did research on our competitors, took notes, tried to learn as much as I could. I was coming in with an outside perspective and with a different outlook from the people who have been there for a long time. I wanted to make a differ-

> Knowledge work is not about what you do but how you do whatever it is you do.

ence there. My feeling was they would welcome the new blood. But when I got there, I felt like all of my ideas were getting shot down. My boss would roll her eyes every time I spoke up in a team meeting, like she just didn't want to hear from me. After a while, it was hard to really care any more."

That eagerness to add value can be very good for business, but it can also be a frustrating distraction for managers. A manager at a beverage distribution warehouse gave me this example: "I've got this one kid, very smart [whom] I hired to unload trucks. On his first day, he came into my office with a list of all these things we are doing wrong. I wanted to say, 'Yeah, great. Now go unload that truck.' I'm glad he is interested in the business and is paying attention to the operation. I'm glad he cares. But most of the people who work here need to move boxes. Lately, when I'm hiring the young guys, I will pass over the ones who seem too smart because not everyone can be an ideas guy here."

Managers often divide their employees—either explicitly or implicitly—into two categories: those who are knowledge workers, or "idea guys," and those who are not. Employees with higher levels of education and responsibility for higher-level tasks are often accorded the status of knowledge workers, while those with lower levels of education and responsibility for lower-level tasks are not. I think this is a big mistake and, unfortunately, a very common one. Sometimes I spend hours trying to get leaders and managers to see that everybody today in a successful organization must be a knowledge worker.

Knowledge work is not about what you do but how you do whatever it is you do. If you work hard to leverage information, technique, and ideas in your job, then you are a knowledge worker—at least in my world. If you don't leverage skill and knowledge in your work to do a better job, you are going to be useless. That's true whether you are digging a ditch or designing the foundation of the building that is going to be built in that ditch.

Most Gen Yers understand this on a gut level and won't have it any other way. The real challenge is to keep them focused on all that work you hired them to do while simultaneously encouraging them to leverage knowledge and skill in that work. The more you encourage Gen Yers to think about their work—whatever that work might be—the more engaged they will be. The more you encourage them to learn while they work, the better they will do their jobs. Whether it's high-tech learning or low tech, help them channel their learning directly into their work instead of shooting down their ideas and dampening their enthusiasm. If you hire someone to unload boxes from a truck and that person wants to be an ideas guy, you need to get that individual to focus his thinking and learning on how to better unload boxes from the truck. If you hire someone to dig a ditch, get that individual to focus on how to dig that ditch better. And so on.

"As soon as they walk in the door, I get them to make an individualized learning plan and keep a learning journal," said a smart manager in a large pharmaceutical company. "They map out their responsibilities, and for each responsibility, I ask them to make a list of learning resources. Those resources can be books, people, Web sites, or really anything else. That alone has yielded some really impressive results. Once they've made that plan, I require them to set learning goals for themselves directly related to their specific responsibilities and journal their learning efforts, how they've tapped each learning resource, what they've learned and how they've used that to improve their performance."

Does this approach work? "They love it," the manager told me. "They get really creative with their learning plans and really get into those journals. I think it improves their performance. The ones who get into it tend to be the most successful—not just working for me, but after they move on." She explained that this approach has particularly helped those trainees—knowledge workers, by any definition—who were always bursting with ideas, suggestions for changes, and improvements for their own responsibilities and those of others. Rather than getting frustrated by their enthusiasm, this manager chose to channel it: "I started encouraging them to also keep track of their good ideas: 'When you have an idea, write it down, sit on it for a couple of weeks, and then revisit it. If it still looks like a good idea to you, think about what it might take to implement it. Do a little research, then make a quick project plan.' This way they are not throwing at us every idea that pops into their heads. I'm taking their ideas seriously, so they take them more seriously. And don't write them off too quickly, because sometimes they come up with great ideas."

When they come in the door, Gen Yers want to hit the ground running. By training them one task a time, giving them the technology tools they need to be fast and efficient, and helping them focus their energy and ideas on the tasks at hand, you'll be able to plug into their enthusiasm and keep their excitement going past their first day on the job.

CHAPTER FOUR

PRACTICE IN LOCO PARENTIS MANAGEMENT

Sure, if my boss was half as cool as my dad, that
would be great!

—*Gen Yer*

A senior private equity managing director told me of a parent call-ing to complain that her son was working too many hours. I asked how he reacted to this call. "I just listened and tried to be polite. I didn't tell her that her son was going to make ten thousand dollars less for every minute she kept me on the phone. But I did the math in my head." He went on, "This is ridiculous. For one thing, my parents never in a million years would have considered calling my boss when I was in my first job out of college. I can't even imagine that. They didn't even know my boss's name. And I would have been mortified if my boss got a call from my parents."

I have heard this story over and over again, in various forms. The details change, but the thrust of the story is always the same. There's no doubt that parents are far more heavily involved in the lives and careers of their young adult children than those of previous generations. College professors and administrators report that the parents of Gen Yers show up to new student orientations in record numbers (some studies indicate that more than 80 percent of new students are now accompanied by a parent for some part or all of orientation). Parents are often consulted several times a day by their college-attending children, using cell phone check-ins to get advice about course choices, classroom protocol, homework assignments, and exams. Professors routinely field parental complaints about student workload and grades. "After all," many parents can be heard saying, "we are paying a lot of money for this education. We *are* the customers here."

This pattern of helicopter parenting carries over once Gen Yers get to the workplace. Managers tell me every day about parents accompanying their children to job interviews and even, once in a while, to the first day of work. Just a cell phone call away, parents are consulted about career decisions and management practices great and small, sometimes all day long. As this Gen Yer put it, "My parents are my best friends. Obviously I'm going to get their take on stuff I'm doing, be it work or whatever. They are right there helping me out no matter what I'm doing. I don't want to be out there on my own. Why would I?" The big surprise comes when managers hear directly from parents, suggesting their children should be working fewer hours, getting different assignments, winning promotions, and receiving pay increases.

Yes, it is commonplace today for parents to insert themselves in support of their young (and not-so-young) adult children, even in the most adult spheres like the workplace where such involvement would have been considered totally inappropriate in the past. But remember, this is nothing new for Gen Yers. Their parents have always been highly engaged with them. Every step of the way, they have been guided, directed, supported, coached, and protected. Unlike previous generations, they don't express much desire to break free as they reach adulthood.

It's become almost cliché to say that Generation Y is overparented. But they are. And that is a fact with which managers today must grapple. "This is an outrage," some managers say, "I shouldn't have to deal with their parents at all." On the flip side, some managers simply accept that their young employees will be accompanied and assisted by their parents throughout the early stages of their working lives. I don't think you should accept that. You hired the employee, not the parents. But you *do* have to deal with it.

One nurse manager on a very busy hospital floor told me, "My approach is simple: sink-or-swim time now, kids. Just let the real world sort them out." The problem is that if you take a sink-or-swim approach with Generation Y employees, they are likely to sink; or go to the shallow end and play; or swim off in their own direction; or get out of the pool, walk across the street, and go work for your competition. And when you hire a replacement, that person is likely to bring his or her parents along too. The irony is that if you hire a Gen Yer who is not close to his or her parents, you may be sorry. Among today's young workers, those who are closest to their parents will probably turn out to be the most able, most achievement oriented, and the hardest working.

In my seminars, I tell managers that the way to deal with the overparenting problem is to take a strong hand as a manager, not a weak one. Your Gen Y employees need to know that you know who they are and care about their success. You need to make it a priority to spend time with them. Guide them through this very difficult and scary world. Break things down for them like a teacher. Provide regular, gentle course corrections to keep them on track. Be honest with them so you can help them improve. Keep close track of their successes no matter how small. Reward the behavior you want and need to see, and even negotiate special rewards for above-and-beyond performance in very small increments along the way.

When I describe this approach in my seminars, often at least one manager will remark, "This sounds a lot like parenting. Are you saying that we should manage these young upstarts as if we are their parents?" I'm afraid the answer I've come to is yes, at least sort of. Let's put it this way. You can't fight the overparenting phenomenon, so run with it. Your Gen Y employees want it. They need it. Without strong management in the workplace, there is a void where their parents have always been.

> **The worst thing you can possibly do with Gen Yers is treat them like children.**

Do be careful and don't get carried away. The worst thing you can possibly do with Gen Yers is treat them like children, talk down to them, or make them feel disrespected. Gen Yers are used to being treated as valued members of the family whose thoughts and feelings are important. Remember, Generation Y has gotten more respect from their parents and elders than any other generation in history.

I call this approach *in loco parentis management*. *In loco parentis*, a Latin term that means "in the place of a parent," typically is used to refer to the position of an institution (usually a school) charged with the care of a minor in the absence of the minor's parent. Step into the void. Take over the tutoring aspects of the parental role in the workplace without taking over the emotional part (at least mostly). Here's what this means:

1. Show them you care.
2. Give them boundaries and structure.
3. Help them keep score.
4. Negotiate special rewards in very small increments.

1. Show Them You Care

When I say, "care about your Gen Yers," I'm not saying you need to love your employees as if they really are your own children or let them come live in your basement. But you may need to usher them through these early stages of their working life and into the next. Help them make the transition.

Don't be alarmed. You don't need to relate to this person's deep inside thoughts, feelings and spirit, or even inner motives. In my view, you shouldn't even try unless you are a trained therapist or pastor. Just care enough to help this person succeed at work, at least whenever this person is working for you. One Gen Yer recently told me, "I need to work for people who know who I am and what I'm doing, and who seem to care. I've had bosses who didn't even know my name. But right now I'm working for this woman who is very busy, but she really connects with me, eye-to-eye kind of, asks me questions and really listens. She's taught me a lot already."

How do you connect with your Gen Yers? First, you have to get to know them as individuals.

Get to Know Them

I don't mean you should learn what's going on in each employee's personal life. Actually I think that's none of your business. Get to know the self each Gen Yer brings to work. Care enough to learn their names. In fact, you should try to use their names a lot. (Gen Yers usually love their own names.) But that's not enough. You need to know who they are at work and what they are doing at any given time:

- How long has Y been working here?
- What is Y's schedule at work?
- What are Y's main tasks every day?
- What are all of Y's other projects?
- Where does Y sit at work? Does Y travel for work? Where?
- Is Y generally a high performer, low performer, or somewhere in the middle?
- Is Y generally a fast worker, slow, or somewhere in the middle?
- Does Y usually get all or most of the details right—or not?
- Is Y generally a positive influence on colleagues, negative, or neutral?
- What is Y's reputation among coworkers?
- How long is Y likely to stay? Is there a chance Y will stay for the long term?

The only way to learn all this information about a Gen Yer is to spend time with him or her one-on-one on a regular basis—helping that person succeed. Of course, some people require more attention than others. But they all need your one-on-one attention. The best way to demonstrate that you care about a Gen Yer's success at work is to invest your own time in helping that person succeed.

Invest the Right Amount of Time with Each Gen Yer

Often managers ask me, "How can I possibly spend meaningful time with every employee, get to know each person, and keep track of what everybody is doing all the time?" The answer depends on how many people you manage. I think you can actually get to know, tune into, and connect in a meaningful way with as many as fifteen or twenty direct reports, but twenty is the limit. (And you'll need to keep notes to keep up with this many.) If you have more than twenty direct reports, you'll have to be selective. But don't make the mistake of spending all of your management time on a few problem employees. Be strategic. Focus on managers first. Anybody you manage who is managing other people should be your first priorities. Second, focus on employees whose work cannot go wrong without great cost or injury to themselves or others—anybody whose work is particularly high stakes, high impact, or dangerous. Third, choose one or two new people each day to spend whatever time you have left. If you do pick two people each day, I recommend picking one from the high end (one star) and one from the low end (one problem). Work your way to the middle of the pack until you have tagged everyone. Then start over and work your way through the list again.

Don't let your one-on-one time with any one person become long and convoluted. You don't have to shoot the breeze. You don't have time to have intense, deep, personal conversations. Keep your one-on-ones relatively brief and focused on preparing the individual for his or her immediate work of the day, week, or month. Help prepare each Gen Yer for the work at hand. Remember, you don't need to show any Gen Yer that you care about him deep inside, only that you care enough about him to spend time setting him up for success.

As you get to know each person, you'll have to fine-tune your approach in every conversation. But start each conversation with these questions: "How are you? What is your top-priority assignment right now? What steps are you following? What step are you on right now? What can I do to help you?" Listen carefully. Then try to wrap up each conversation with some concrete actionable advice.

"I try to have a particular goal that I'm working toward with every person," said a manager in a major engineering firm. "Every person is a different situation. With one person, I'm always trying to move her along on a particular matter, finishing up one step and moving on to the next. With another person, I try to help him slow down and pay attention to the details. With another person it might be tuck in your shirt, come to work on time, stop talking on the phone all the time. But I'm always working toward a particular goal with every person, and they know I really care about their success."

Don't Pretend

I realize that this chapter is called "Practice In Loco Parentis Management," but don't get me wrong. I am not saying you should actually pretend to be a parent to your employees at work. In fact, you shouldn't pretend anything. Gen Yers have giant BS detectors, especially around authority figures. You have to be authentic to succeed with them. So focus on the authentic common interest between you two, which is the work at hand, and on playing very well the real role you have in their working lives: that of a manager.

You are running a workplace. The relationships at work are transactional relationships. I promise you, none of your employees would be showing up to work every day if you were not paying them. So treat each person and the relationship with respect. But don't hesitate to take charge and tell them what to do. You are paying them to work very well, very fast, all day long. Make that fact explicit, keep a spotlight on it, and never try to camouflage it.

One Gen Yer put it plainly: "People can be so fraudulent around here. You know what? Don't humor me."

Some managers unfortunately pretend to be friends with their employees. I realize plenty of workplace friendships are genuine. But let's face it: when you have a genuine friendship with a colleague at work, especially a direct report whom you are supposed to be managing, you try to keep friendship separate from work. Deep friendships are the ones you protect from the complications of the workplace and sometimes, in private, you almost have to do some apologizing for your cool demeanor in the workplace. If you don't have a genuine friendship with an employee, don't try to play Mr. Friend at work. It is often confusing and sometimes damaging. One Gen Yer put it plainly: "People can be so fraudulent around here. You know what? Don't humor me. I get it. You're in charge. I'm fine with that. Stop wasting my time pretending to be my best friend. Tell me what you want me to do. Go ahead and tell it like it is."

Often managers tell me, "I think the younger employees like me. They think I'm pretty cool. I don't want to spoil that." This hope sometimes leads managers to build rapport on unhealthy ground. Sometimes these managers will participate in bad-mouthing the larger organization or the powers that be, blaming higher-ups for unpopular decisions, letting employees off the hook on requirements, and looking the other way when people mess up. These managers might be tempted to make promises they can't keep, give employees more responsibility than they can handle, and offer insincere praise. Often these managers give Gen Yers the false impression that their input will be included in decisions when it won't be. They don't make it clear where the employee's discretion begins and where it ends, and this sometimes leads young employees to go off wildly in their own direction thinking that is exactly what they are supposed to be doing. Avoid these giant pitfalls.

I'm not suggesting you shouldn't be cordial and friendly with your employees. I don't mean you shouldn't be polite. I'm suggesting that you build rapport with employees by talking about the real stuff you have in common, which is the work at hand. The more you focus your relationship on work, the better the work will go. You will prevent unnecessary problems and solve problems before they get out of control.

Sometimes managers try to turn themselves into cheerleaders in an attempt to imitate those very rare individuals who have that special ability to inspire: charisma, contagious passion, and infectious enthusiasm. Is this really you? If it is, then you are blessed. But if that is not you, you simply cannot learn it, and you shouldn't waste your time trying. Lead, but don't pretend to be a cheerleader. Sympathize, but don't pretend to be a therapist. Be authoritative, but don't pretend to be a tyrant. You can lead in a demanding and supportive way and be real all at the same time.

"After years of trying on one management personality after another, I finally realized that the only personality that works on me is my own," one wise retail manager told me. "I am naturally pushy and enthusiastic, and that's how I talk to my people. I have to impose that patience and discipline on myself to make sure I take my time and spell things out for them in a way they understand. Now I spend a lot more time thinking about exactly what I need to communicate to people and making sure expectations are clear. Doing that is what gives me the patience and discipline. But I'm going to be pushy and enthusiastic. That's just who I am."

Choose your words carefully. By all means, be your best self. But be yourself.

2. Give Them Structure and Boundaries

The Gen Yers you manage want freedom to maneuver at work. They want some latitude when it comes to their schedule, where they do their work, whom they work with, what they do, and how they do it. The problem is that every task, responsibility, and project has parameters that constrain every employee's freedom.

And as much as they love freedom, Gen Yers also gravitate to structure and boundaries. For one thing, they don't want to waste their time. Don't forget, since they were kids, Gen Yers have been hyperscheduled by overbearing adults. Whether they were being subjected to metal detectors, locker searches and lockdowns in school, or their own "individual learning plans"—and everything in between—Gen Yers are well accustomed to programs and procedures. One Gen Yer describes it this way: "The last thing I'm looking for is somebody telling me, 'Yeah, do it how you think it should be done,' but then it turns out she already knows exactly how she wants it done. I don't want to beat my head against the wall trying to figure something out if you've already got it figured out. I definitely am interested in putting my personal stamp on things, but if that's not going to happen, tell me up front."

If you want to give Gen Yers more freedom at work, the biggest favor you can do for them is establish clear boundaries and give them a structure within which they can function with some autonomy. It is true that some jobs require employees to take risks and make mistakes. Even in those cases, it is the manager's job to help Gen Yers avoid taking unnecessary risks and repeating mistakes that others have already made. Creativity and innovation do not require recklessness. You tell the advertising copywriter to "think outside the box," but you must also help him avoid libel, slander, and obscenity. You need the nuclear scientist to be innovative, but you must help her avoid a nuclear explosion. It's great if your food preparation workers are creative, but you don't want them changing the recipes on regular menu items. As a leader, you have to create a structure and clear boundaries in order to create a space in which risk taking and mistakes are truly safe in the context of the job.

Often a good way to allow Gen Yers to express creativity is to give them assignments that are truly matters of first impression. Maybe you, as the manager, don't yet have a clear goal in mind; you don't know exactly what you are looking for yet. This is a great opportunity to ask a young employee to "take a crack at it" and "do it however you think it should be done" and really mean what you say. It's perfectly fine to use Gen Yers to help you work out the early stages of your own creative process. But make sure you are clear from the start about the structure and boundaries. Explain that you are delegating only the initial stage of the creative process and you intend to take the project back.

In fact, whenever you have a new task, responsibility, or project for one of your very capable young employees, you should always start by spelling out expectations. Make absolutely sure that person understands exactly what he is expected to do and how he is expected to do it. That's the only way to get employees to adopt your organization's best practices and turn them into standard operating procedures. As long as the assignment lasts, you should follow up regularly with one-on-one check-in conversations to review the employee's progress. In those conversations, you should ask, "What have you already done? What steps did you follow? What step are you going to do next?" Listen carefully to their answers. Make it a habit to wrap up these conversations by deciding on a specific place and time for your next meeting to follow up.

Every assignment, no matter how much freedom and creativity is required, must have clear goals and specific deadlines with measurable benchmarks along the way. Boundaries and structure, however loose, are actually the keys to making freedom and creativity in the real world possible.

3. Help Them Keep Score

You might think a generation raised on mantras like "we're all winners" and "everyone gets a trophy" wouldn't be particularly competitive. But that is not the case. While the self-esteem movement was chipping away at Generation Yers' competitiveness, the testing movement was building it back up. Still, testing breeds a different kind of competitiveness: competition against standards and benchmarks, against averages and means, and against one's own past performance.

Think about a video game that a Gen Yer might practice and practice, beating one high score after another, set by himself. He wins every time, and nobody has a reason to feel bad. That's the kind of competition Gen Yers are looking for: they want to compete against themselves in a safe environment where they can try over and over again to improve on their own performance benchmarks. When it comes to competitiveness at work, this is what one Gen Yer had to say: "I'll do whatever they want me to do. Just tell me someone is keeping track of all this stuff I'm doing. Tell me I'm getting credit for it, that I've been racking up points here like mad. Tell me someone is keeping score."

When Gen Yers know you are keeping track of their day-to-day performance, their measuring instinct is sparked and their competitive spirit ignited. Keeping close track of their work tells them that they are important and their work is important. The process motivates them to perform because they want to get credit, score points, earn more of whatever there is to earn.

"I was managing this very young team of programmers," a senior manager in one of our nation's intelligence agencies started to tell me. "For the first few months, our weekly team meetings were great, but after every meeting, the programmers would come up to me one by one asking for feedback on their individual work. I kept trying to address this in the team meetings by asking each of them for status reports in our meetings. But one by one, they would come see me after the meeting to ask for individual feedback. Finally, in one of the team meetings, I asked the group about it point-blank. They all said, 'We all want to know how we are doing, individually.' So I said to them joking, 'Do you want me to give out gold stars when you do a good job?' And they all nodded affirmatively. They were very cheerful about it, but I was having a hard time with it. But I started giving out gold stars to them, individually, in the team meetings, and they loved it. They started asking all the time, 'Do I get a gold star for that?'"

> Gen Yers want to compete against themselves in a safe environment.

I've heard stories like this over and over again from managers of Gen Yers in a whole range of industries. Yes, they want to earn gold stars. Just remember that if you are going to give out gold stars or points of any kind, you have to make it very clear every step of the way exactly how those points can be earned—or lost. You need a system.

The Point System

One outstanding system I've seen in action is used in the warehouse of a large beverage wholesaler. Every day, hundreds (or even thousands) of boxes come in one end of the warehouse and hundreds more go out the other end. All day long, boxes are being moved from one end to the other, meticulously accounted for by bar codes scanned each time they are moved. Everybody in that warehouse is on a point system. One of the warehouse managers told me, "The only way you get points around here is moving boxes. If you drive a delivery truck, you get points by delivering boxes. You break bottles, you lose points. If you work in the loading dock, you get points by loading boxes onto the truck. Points are how everything gets done here. That's how you make extra money. That's how you get to leave early or get extra days off." How does the system work? The warehouse manager laughed: "Everybody is always trying to get points, especially the young guys. We've got a very young group in the warehouse. These guys are practically climbing over each other when a truck pulls in. The young guys want to get their points. Some of them want to work all day and make more money. Some of them just want to get their points and get out of here for the day. But they all want to get those points. I just sit back and let [the points] do most of the management work."

Similarly, the founding partner of a small advertising firm told me that she started giving out "extra points" to associates "for above-and-beyond performance on very difficult projects." She told me, "At first, I didn't even know what I really meant by extra points. But I'd usually come back with a bonus check, so the points came to mean something." The practice was so popular among the younger associates that the partner started attaching points to projects in advance. "After a while, just about any task, no matter how small, was eligible for extra points. If you get something done very fast, you might get extra points. If you really do a fantastic job on something, that's extra points. It's for above-and-beyond performance. And it's worth money."

Am I saying you should create a point system or start giving out gold stars to your Gen Yers? If you can think of easy ways to convert the performance you need from your young employees into a point system, then maybe you should consider it. I promise you, a point system will get Gen Yers focused like a laser beam. If you want them to start showing up earlier for work, attach points for every minute they arrive early, and take away points for every minute they come in late. If you want Gen Yers to meet quality standards, give them checklists of every detail and specification, and give points for every detail and specification completed—and take away points for every one missed. If you want Gen Yers to speed up, set a realistic quota of tasks per hour and give points for every task done over the quota—and take away points for every task under the quota. And so on.

Keeping Track Informally

Formal gold stars and point systems are not always necessary. You will get a similar result as long as you make it clear that you are paying close attention to what they are doing and keeping score, one way or another. Have regular one-on-one conversations where you ask for an account of what the person has done since your last conversation: "What concrete actions did you take? Did you meet the expectations we spelled out? Did you do all the items on your to-do list?" Then offer credit for the items done and take note of the items not yet done. You might say, "You did a great job on A, B, and C. But on D, you fell a little short. So that's three out of four for today. Let's talk about how you are going to do D next."

Another approach is to help Gen Yers keep track of their own work by using self-monitoring tools like project plans, checklists, and activity logs. Gen Yers can monitor whether they are meeting goals and deadlines laid out in a project plan, make notations within checklists, and report to you at regular intervals. Activity logs are diaries that Gen Yers can keep, noting contemporaneously exactly what they do all day, including breaks and interruptions. Each time he or she moves on to a new activity, the Gen Yer might note the time and the new activity. By using these tools, Gen Yers can document their own hard work every step of the way and build their own track record of success.

4. Negotiate Special Rewards in Very Small Increments

Today we live in a world in which relationships are governed by an increasingly short-term and transactional logic. That's true for people of all ages. But Gen Yers have never known it any other way. Segmented as a market from birth and armed with credit cards, they have been taught to think of themselves as customers in virtually every sphere. Even in their roles as students, most Gen Yers think of themselves as buying and consuming the learning services sold by schools. Meanwhile, their parents have been negotiating "choices" with them since they first uttered "I want" as toddlers, trading short-term rewards for short-term desired behavior.

By the time Gen Yers arrive at the workplace, short-term transactional thinking is second nature to them. They are still thinking like customers. Sometimes when I point this out to managers, they'll say, "Yeah, well, they're not paying us. We are paying them. So what currency do they bring to the transaction? They can do as they are told." I agree with that 100 percent.

Of course, you want to get more work and better work out of every one of your Gen Yers. For their part, Gen Yers want to earn more of what they need and want. The best solution? Plug into Gen Yers' transactional mind-set. Stop paying them and start *buying* their results, one by one. The more you trade results for rewards, the more reliable their performance will be. The smaller the increments you buy in, the more effective it will be. "I had this manager who would always say to me, 'What do you need from me?' a Gen Yer told me. "I'd always know she was going to get me back with,

'Great. Here's what I need from you.' She did that with everybody. She knew I needed the money and went out of her way to help me make more money, which was really great of her."

The critical element when it comes to rewarding Gen Yers is letting them know that rewards are tied to concrete actions within their own direct control. This might remind you of the old-fashioned pay scheme called piecework in which individuals are paid an agreed-on amount for each defined unit of work they produce. The seamstress might be paid per stitch or per finished garment. The accountant might be paid per tax return prepared. The computer programmer might be paid per line of new code written. And so on. The key to your success will be defining those measurable pieces of work and setting a price per piece.

Traditional Compensation Versus Short-Term Rewards

"Oh yeah?" one manager interrupted to ask in the middle of one of my seminars, "Then why do Gen Yers push so hard for more when it comes to traditional compensation and benefits? It's not like they are saying, 'Don't give me health care, don't give me the 401k, and don't give me the salary. I'll just take the short-term rewards.' Are you telling me they just want more of everything?"

This was no doubt a fair question and one that is on the minds of a lot of managers. Perhaps if given the choice, many Gen Yers would actually opt for a safe lifelong employment relationship with secure, long-term vesting rewards. The problem is that you won't find any Gen Yers who actually believe that this is a real option in today's world. To them, it sounds like an absurd claim on its face—largely because it is. Therefore, most Gen Yers are concerned about all the rewards they might be able to extract from their immediate boss in the short term. However, Gen Yers are also acutely aware that the compensation systems and language of their employers almost always revolve around the traditional elements of compensation and benefits; pay scales or salary, health care plans, eligibility for 401k or pension plans, and the like. They often ask about traditional rewards because they are aware that you only know how to talk about traditional rewards—they figure at least the conversation will make sense to you. They also want you to think they care about the reward system you seem to care so much about. Plus, they figure they might as well get everything they can out of that system, even as they are making their other more idiosyncratic requests.

> Most Gen Yers are concerned about all the rewards they might be able to extract from their immediate boss in the short term.

The answer, then, is, sure, they want more of everything. But the real performance drivers for Gen Yers are the short-term, special rewards you negotiate in exchange for their short-term above-and-beyond performance. A senior engineer shared this story with me: "One of the engineers on my team, a young lady who talked about little else but flextime and work-life balance, pretty much dropped everything for two months and lived here around the clock working on a killer deadline for me. Why? I arranged for her to take six weeks off, two unpaid, in a row after the project was finished. That was all it took. She was here around the clock for two months, then she disappeared for six weeks and came back happy as could be. The other two guys on that team? They just wanted a bonus check." He concluded, "They all want something different. But they all want something, and most of them are willing to work for it."

Negotiating Rewards in Small Increments

So when that Gen Yer knocks on your office door and asks if you have a minute to discuss his special need or want, you could roll your eyes and think about beating your head against the wall—or you could realize that this need or want might just be the key to driving this employee's performance to a whole new level, or at least the key to getting more work out of him better and faster for the short term.

The best approach is to negotiate these special rewards in very small increments. You want to be able to say, "Okay. I'll do that for you tomorrow if you do X for me today." Work a particularly unde-sirable shift? Work longer hours? Work with a difficult team? Do some heavy lifting? Work in some out of the way location? Clean up some unpleasant mess? Then deliver the reward in question as soon as you possibly can. Immediate rewards are much more effec-tive with Gen Yers because they provide a greater sense of control and a higher level of reinforcement. Gen Yers are likely to remem-ber the precise details and context of the performance and are therefore more likely to make the connection the next time the desired performance is called for. Plus they won't spend time won-dering if their performance has been noted and appreciated, and they will therefore be less likely to lose the momentum generated by their short-term success.

Most managers have more discretionary resources at their dis-posal than they realize. These are often resources that can be de-ployed as special short-term rewards. What extra funds are available to you that you might be able to use for special short-term bonuses? What can you do to improve work conditions in the short term for your employees? How much latitude do you have to make special short-term accommodations in employees' schedules or paid time off? How much control do you have over extra training opportuni-ties? Can you offer exposure to decision makers? How hard is it to have a written commendation added to an employee's file? There are many extra rewards managers have in their control, and you need to use every resource at your disposal.

That does *not* mean that everything is open to negotiation. You should be rock solid on your basic standards and requirements. What is not negotiable? What is essential? What is not acceptable? That's your starting point. From there, take control of the ongoing negotiation and help Gen Yers earn those special rewards they want so much. In the process, you'll get so much more, and better, and faster work out of them, one day at a time.

CHAPTER FIVE

GIVE THEM THE GIFT OF CONTEXT

At the orientation, they went on and on about how this is my company now too. They want me to feel like I am an owner of the company. They said they look at us as "internal customers." Then I get in trouble for talking too much in the first team meeting. My supervisor tells me, "You've only been here for two weeks; maybe you should just hold your comments and pay attention." I didn't appreciate that too much.

—Gen Yer

The following story was told to me by a senior executive in a large automobile parts supply company: "We were downsizing the organization, but we were trying to do it through controlled attrition. So we were offering buyouts for senior people in certain categories who were willing and able to leave the company inside of twelve months. When the younger people got wind of this, we were inundated with requests from them. They wanted to know why they were not being offered the buyout. I fielded some of these requests myself so I had a chance to say, 'But you are ineligible.' They would say, 'Why?' I'd say, 'You've been here less than a year.'

And they would say, 'So?' They honestly didn't get why they were in a different position from the employees who had been here for twenty or thirty years."

We see this sort of thing in our research all the time. Managers often tell us that their Gen Yers suffer from a fundamental lack of context. This is partly a life stage issue: younger people have less life experience than older people and thus fewer points of reference to compare circumstances, people, and relationships. Context is all about these points of reference. So lack of context goes with the territory when it come to young employees.

Still, Gen Yers' lack of context seems to stem from more than just youth and inexperience. "When I was young and inexperienced," said a fifty-something sales manager in a pharmaceutical company, "I may have been cocky, but I knew age and experience mattered and I knew I didn't have either. Recently I set a new guy up with some paperwork. When I came back a few hours later to check on him, he was gone. I looked across the hallway and realized he had set himself up in a different cube than the one I put him in. I asked him what he was doing, and he told me that he liked the other cube better. Of course, you like that one better. That one is bigger, has a window, and a bigger desk. That's why it goes to someone who's been here more than six hours. It's like they don't even realize that some of us have been working here since they were in diapers. They don't see it, or they just don't see why it matters."

In fact, our research shows that Gen Yers do appreciate and respect age and experience. After all, they have enjoyed the most nurturing relationships with adults perhaps of any generation in recorded history. But their appreciation and respect don't translate into deference or acquiescence. Gen Yers have grown up in a child-centric era in which their feelings, words, and actions have usually been accorded a huge amount of respect by the adults in their lives. Their relationships with adults have rarely been defined in terms of authority and have instead often been inflected by familiarity. Gen Yers' preferences have been given much weight, and their opinions and words have been given much airtime in discussions. Misbehavior has been more and more likely diagnosed instead of punished. And their accomplishments have been highlighted with a lot of emphasis.

As the sales manager for the pharmaceutical company put it, "Nobody has ever said to them, 'Because I said so!' It's like they exist in a vacuum. Nobody has ever pulled them aside and said to them, 'Look, we've been at this for a long time. This is how we do things around here. You've just arrived. This is where you fit in to our picture.'"

I believe he is on to something.

Giving Gen Yers the Gift of Context

Giving Gen Yers the gift of context means explaining that no matter who that Gen Yer may be, what he wants to achieve, or how he wants to behave, his role in any situation is determined in large part by factors that have nothing to do with him. There are preexisting, independent factors that would be present even if he were not, and they determine the context of any situation.

Context is easier to understand when we consider extreme examples of it: jail, war, famine, earthquakes. In any of these contexts, the possibilities are limited, and so is the scope of an individual's potential role. In these contexts, certain expectations, hopes, expressions, and actions are inappropriate. While it is relatively easy to be sensitive to extreme contexts, it is often difficult for people, Gen Yers in particular, to be sensitive to more subtle contexts, particularly when they walk into new situations. Every situation has a context that limits possibilities and limits the scope of an individual's potential role.

The big mistake leaders and managers often make is allowing Gen Yers to remain in their vacuum. Telling Gen Yers all about the company is not the same as giving them context. Telling Gen Yers, "This is how it was for me when I was a new employee," is not giving them context. Understanding context is about understanding where one fits in the larger picture.

> The big mistake leaders and managers often make is allowing Gen Yers to remain in their vacuum. Telling Gen Yers all about the company is not the same as giving them context.

In our career seminars, we teach Gen Yers to use a simple brainstorming tool in order to situate themselves in a new context, and you can use it to teach your Gen Yers. We tell them that before they can figure out where they fit in an organization, they need to get a handle on the other pieces of the puzzle. We ask them to think about and respond to the following questions:

- Where am I? What is this place?
- What is going on here? What is the mission of the group?
- Why is everybody here? What is at stake for the group and for each person in the group?
- When did they all get here?
- Who are all these people? What role does each person play?
- How are they accustomed to doing things around here? What is standard operating procedure for them?
- Why am I here?
- What is at stake for me?
- When did I get here?
- What is my appropriate role in relation to the other people in the group?
- What is my appropriate role in relation to the mission? Who am I in this context?

Teach Them to ~~Play~~ Work Well with Others

Conflicts, dislikes, and gripes between and among employees are very common and can be some of the most difficult issues for managers. We see this in our research all the time. Cliques, in particular, are a common problem in the workplace. They always have been. Gen Yers, brand new to a workplace, are often lured into cliques or distracting personal relationships by one social ringleader or another. As one Gen Yer put it: "My boss was sort of nonpresent most of the time at work. I got most of my cues from the other people I was working with. One of the ladies at work, I connected with her right away. She told me who was cool and who to stay away from. I would definitely say we became friends." When this happens, the Gen Yer's focus is drawn away from the work and onto personal and social machinations. How can managers deal with this problem?

When Gen Yers say that their most important relationship at work is with their immediate manager, they have many fewer personal conflicts with other employees at work. We have also found that the busier Gen Yers are with their tasks and responsibilities at work, the more they tend to build their workplace relationships with colleagues around shared or dovetailing tasks and responsibilities (as opposed to personal matters). As a result, their workplace relationships tend to be more professional.

As a manager, the best thing you can do is help Gen Yers anticipate relationship dynamics that are likely to cause conflict and help them prepare for those situations. Our research indicates the four issues that most often cause relationship conflicts for Gen Yers at work. Prepare them in advance to handle these issues.

Issue #1: The Multiple Boss Problem

In many organizations, Gen Yers answer to more than one boss. That means they have to balance competing demands for their time and energy. When you give a Gen Yer an assignment, it may not always be clear how many other assignments he is juggling at that point. Are you interfering with assignments from other bosses? Will another assignment come up from another boss and interfere with your assignment? The problem is that Gen Yers feel as if they are stuck in the middle. Sometimes they try to please everybody and end up pleasing nobody. Other times they try to choose for themselves which assignment is a priority. Maybe they choose the assignment from the boss who seems most important to them. Or maybe they choose the assignment from the boss they like the best. Or maybe they try to make a business judgment about which assignment should take precedence. But this complicated situation often gets them into trouble with one or more of their bosses.

How can you help them avoid this problem?

Step one: When you give Gen Yers assignments, always ask for an inventory of all their other assignments at that moment. That way, if you or another manager becomes aware of a potential conflict, you can help the Gen Yer resolve it there and then.

Step two: Explain the problem to Gen Yers in advance, and give them standard operating procedures for dealing with it. Teach them, when they receive assignments, to first give the assigning manager an inventory of all other assignments so that potential conflicts can be resolved in advance. When potential conflicts do arise, teach them not to try to resolve the conflicts. Rather, they should immediately contact each competing boss and ask for help resolving the conflict.

Issue #2: The Chain-of-Command Problem

Sometimes Gen Yers resist their immediate manager's authority or find their immediate manager to be unhelpful or unresponsive to their requests. Or sometimes Gen Yers disagree with the immediate manager's decisions. In these cases, Gen Yers often try to go around their immediate manager and seek to deal directly with their manager's manager or their manager's manager's manager. After all, the manager's manager's manager is more powerful, probably more experienced, has more access to resources, and may even be more responsive. Obviously, when Gen Yers end-run this immediate manager, they are likely to encounter increased relationship stress with that manager as well as their coworkers.

How can you help them avoid this problem?

Step one: Teach them to deal with their immediate managers whenever possible. If they are unable to get what they need from their immediate manager, teach them under what circumstances to request a meeting with their immediate manager *and* their manager's manager together.

> Gen Yers sometimes feel they are treated with disrespect by their older, more experienced colleagues.

This will raise the gravity of end-running the chain of command and lead them to do it only when it's really necessary.

Step two: When Gen Yers end-run their immediate managers, whomever they try to deal with instead should immediately bring the Gen Yer's immediate manager into the loop and make the conversation a three-way conversation. The exception is a meeting requested in confidence, in which case someone from HR should be included.

Issue #3: The Older, More Experienced Colleagues Problem

Sometimes Gen Yers rub older more experienced colleagues the wrong way because they seem so eager to take on responsibilities, prove themselves, and do things in newfangled ways. These more experienced colleagues can also become resentful when managers accede to Gen Yers' demands for rapid advancement or special accommodations and rewards. But the most common complaint we hear is that older, more experienced colleagues believe Gen Yers do not accord them an appropriate degree of respect and deference. Meanwhile, Gen Yers sometimes feel they are treated with disrespect by their older, more experienced colleagues.

How can you help Gen Yers avoid this problem?

Step one: Remind them that their older, more experienced colleagues are older and more experienced. Consider assigning each Gen Yer an older, more experienced person as a peer adviser. Although the peer advisers may have no official authority in the relationships, the peer adviser role creates one-on-one relationships of trust and confidence and mutual respect between Gen Yers and their older colleagues. It is very important that these relationships not be pro forma, but rather that a concrete business purpose be attached to the relationship.

Step two: If you assign special responsibilities, award fast-track promotions, or make accommodations or rewards available to Gen Yers, then you should make a serious effort to make them equally available to older, more experienced workers too. Any special treatment should be available to older and younger workers alike and always in exchange for meeting clear, measurable performance expectations.

Issue #4: Depending on Employees in Other Teams, Departments or Divisions, or Even Outside Vendors

These interdependencies cause relationship conflicts when Gen Yers have a hard time getting what they need out of other employees and thus aren't able to complete their own tasks and responsibilities properly or in a timely fashion.

How can you help them avoid this problem?

Step one: Teach Gen Yers to focus on tasks they can accomplish on their own while they are waiting for whatever it is they need from other employees.

Step two: Teach Gen Yers exactly how to work the system and how to interact more effectively with these people in order to get more of what they need faster from other people. Give them good standard operating procedures for spelling out their needs and asking for clear deliverables with specific timetables; and obtaining commitments and following up at regular intervals without seeming as if they are pestering.

Step three: Teach them when and how to bring in you or another authority figure in order to apply extra pressure when necessary.

Teach Them How to Shine in Presentations and Meetings

A training manager in a large insurance company shared this story with me: "My assistant helped me prepare for a presentation to a senior vice president who is an internal customer. She wanted to come in to the meeting with me, which I said was fine. But throughout my presentation, she kept interrupting to explain, 'I prepared the slide show,' or 'Let me explain this cost estimate I prepared,' or 'I think maybe you should let me answer this question.'" She continued, "After the meeting, I was getting ready to tell her how inappropriate her conduct had been, but she beat me to the punch. She said, 'Listen, if I'm going to do all the work for a presentation like that, I'd really prefer it if you just let me make the presentation alone. I'd really prefer if you weren't in the meeting. Next time, could I just go solo?' I was speechless. I really didn't know what I was supposed to say."

What was she supposed to say? Whenever your Gen Yers have to—or want to—attend meetings or give a presentation as part of their responsibilities at work, you need to prepare them rigorously in advance. The most important thing you can do for them is clarify whether a presentation or meeting is indeed a primary opportunity for them to shine or impress people *or not*. Here are four other best practices for how to behave in presentations and meetings that you really should teach Gen Yers:

1. Before attending any meeting or presentation, make sure you know what the meeting is about and whether your attendance is required, requested, or at least acceptable. Do you need to attend? Should you attend?

2. Prepare in advance. Is there any material you should review or read before the meeting? Are there any conversations you need

to have before the meeting? Are there any work products you need to prepare before the meeting?

3. Identify exactly what your role in the meeting is. Who are you representing in that meeting? What information are you responsible for communicating? What information are you responsible for gathering? If you are not a primary actor in the meeting, often the best thing you can do is say as little as possible and practice good meeting manners. Come one minute early, and sit quietly until the meeting begins. When the meeting starts, speak only when you are asked a question directly. Pay attention and take notes. If you are tempted to speak up, bite your tongue. Write a very quick note to yourself so you don't lose your thought. But don't stop listening. Does your point still need to be raised? Is it a point that everyone needs to hear, right here and now? If you have a question, could it be asked at a later time, off-line, when everyone is not trapped in this meeting? Or is it a question that everyone needs answered here and now?

4. If you are the one making a presentation, then prepare like crazy. Ask yourself exactly what value you have to offer the group. Never start working on the slide shows and handouts first. Instead, start with a script for yourself. and rehearse it. And then rehearse some more. Only then, if you have time and if it will be helpful to the group, create prepared materials to accompany your words.

Finally, sometimes meetings are often called for no good reason and *are* a waste of time. In those meetings, teach Gen Yers not to say a single word that will unnecessarily lengthen the meeting.

Teach Them How to Deal with Your Boss's Boss's Boss and Other Big Shots

One Gen Yer says, "You want me to act all impressed? Be impressive. What can I say? If you are the big guy around here, then of course I'm going to set my sights on you. But you are still just another person. You know what they say: 'Everybody poops.' Don't get all high and mighty with me."

A senior official in a U.S. government agency says: "They have no respect for authority." He paused and then clarified: "Well, they do and they don't. If they think you can help their career, then they want to know you. In fact, they will beat down your door to get your attention. But I say they have no respect for authority because they are not intimidated by titles at all. I want to tell them that if this person is impressive enough that you are trying to get her attention, then she is impressive enough that you should be deferent toward her. I mean, you don't just go up to her and say, 'Hey, how's it goin'?'"

So what *is* going on here? Gen Yers may not know exactly how to pay proper respect to those in positions of authority, but I promise you, they know well that powerful decision makers can help them. And they know that building relationships with powerful decision makers is a key to accelerating career success. If anything, Gen Yers are more attuned than those of other generations to the value of so-called networking because they have been accustomed since childhood to building close relationships with parents, teachers, and counselors in all dimensions of their lives.

This inclination is especially notable among the most ambitious Gen Yers—those at the highest end of the achievement spectrum. Smart leaders and managers learn to tap into Gen Yers' desire for networking opportunities and use that desire for extra leverage by making exposure to senior leaders a reward for high performance. For all of the upsides of this approach, however, it often leads to unintended consequences.

Several executives in a major insurance company have told me different versions of this story. It seems that this company, like so many others, has a fast-track program for high-potential entry-level Gen Yers. Although there are many different aspects to this fast-track program, one component is exposing the young employees to C-level executives. These fast-trackers spend time in small groups and in one-on-one meetings with the CEO of the company, the chief financial officer, the chief operating officer, as well as the executive vice presidents.

> Gen Yers know well that powerful decision makers can help them.

These are meant to be interactive discussion sessions, sometimes over lunch or at cocktail parties. Typically the senior executives participating in these sessions go out of their way to seem accessible: they try to engage with the young employees, use their names, answer questions, and ask them to share their impressions and opinions. Often the senior executives wrap up these encounters by saying something like, "I want you to stay in touch with me. I want to know how things are going for you. I want to know if you need something. Here is my e-mail address. Here is my assistant's direct line."

So what's the problem? According to one of the leaders of this fast-track program, "The problem is that the fast-trackers take them up on it!" Gen Yers who come out of the fast-track program "think nothing of calling the CEO or e-mailing him" to tell him "they don't like their work space, they are unhappy with an assignment, they don't like their boss" or "to get special approval for something their boss has told them they couldn't do." But isn't that one of the intentions of the fast-track program: To give these high-potential Gen Yers a feeling of access to and connection with senior executives? "Yes," said one of these executives. "But they are so inappropriate about it. They aren't supposed to get the idea that they are best friends with the CEO. Sometimes you find them bragging to more experienced people, like, 'I know the CEO,' or even threatening their boss: 'I'm going to tell the CEO about this.' That is most definitely *not* our intention. It makes the program look bad. It's also embarrassing to the fast-tracker, even if he or she doesn't realize it."

How do you give high-potential and high-performing Gen Yers exposure to decision makers who can help them without exposing everybody involved to this type of embarrassing situation? You need to give Gen Yers context: explain to them exactly who they should be reaching out to (and not), for what reasons, when, and how.

In our career seminars, we teach a number of basic techniques for building relationships with big-shot decision makers. Teach these techniques to your young employees:

1. Don't waste the time of busy people. Don't bother networking unless you have a very good reason—a real and appropriate

business reason to transact. Don't try to make up a reason. If you do that, then any relationship you might build will be disingenuous.

2. Always approach decision makers with what you have to offer, not what you need or want. Clarify exactly what it is you have to offer this person that is real and valuable and that she cannot get easily from another source. If you don't have something real and valuable and special to offer, then you are probably not ready to reach out to that decision maker.

3. Do some homework before making contact. Make sure you are reaching out to the right decision maker: Is this person prepared to engage in the transaction you propose? If you talk to the service manager in a car dealership, no matter what you say, she is not going to sell you a car, although she will be glad to make arrangements to have your car fixed. If you want to buy a car, you need to talk to a salesperson. You don't e-mail the CEO if you need a new stapler.

4. Win over the gatekeepers. Many of the people you want to reach will be insulated from the outside world by assistants who carefully guard their time and attention. These assistants screen voice mail, e-mail, paper mail, faxes, overnight packages, and any other communications before their bosses ever see them. That makes these gatekeepers very powerful. No matter how many times you call, write, fax, e-mail, and send something overnight, if the gatekeeper doesn't want you to get through, you probably won't. But gatekeepers are people too. And if you want their help, you have to recognize them as individuals and take the time to build relationships with them. First, identify the real gatekeeper by asking good questions: "Do you check Ms. Jones's voice mail, or does she check it herself?" Or, "Do you keep Mr. Smith's schedule, or does he keep it himself?" Once you have identified the real gatekeeper, treat that person with the same measure of respect and deference you would accord the decision maker you are trying to reach. Teach the gatekeeper your name by using multiple contacts addressed directly to the gatekeeper. Send a letter, voice mail, fax, and e-mail, all at the same time thanking the gatekeeper for taking the time to talk with you. Don't even mention the decision maker

in this round of communication. Follow up with a phone call, and see if the gatekeeper remembers you. If so, then it's time to ask the gatekeeper to raise the gate and let you in: "What would be the best way to get an e-mail directly to Ms. Jones?" "How can I make sure that Mr. Smith will get my memo?" When you win over the gatekeeper, you will get past the gate.

5. Once you get on the radar screen, prove you are more than just a blip. Demonstrate your value immediately by making the words you say and any materials you send interesting and useful. That means you may have to write a script and rehearse or do some work in advance on speculation and hope for the chance to share it.

6. Finally, if you have a successful contact, you should conclude by asking the decision maker how she wants to proceed with the relationship. Once you get the ball rolling, you don't want to be the one to let it drop. But you don't want to be a pest either. If the relationship is hot (you just submitted a proposal), then your follow-ups should be frequent (once a week). If the relationship isn't going anywhere right away (maybe the person said to you, "I'll get back to you if I am interested"), then your follow-ups should be less frequent (every other month). If you are not sure, then ask, listen carefully, and act accordingly.

> The key is to help Gen Yers figure out where they fit in an organization.

Gen Yers have particular difficulty tuning in to new contexts at work and realizing how context often restricts the range of their appropriate behavior. Whether you are helping Gen Yers reach out to higher-ups and decision makers, conduct themselves properly in meetings, or avoid the most common relationship conflicts, the key is to help them learn to ask themselves, "Where do I fit in this situation?"

CHAPTER SIX

GET THEM TO CARE ABOUT GREAT CUSTOMER SERVICE

I get that they really want us to kiss every customer's
ass and swallow my pride and pretend I really care.
Rest assured, if this were my business, I'd feel the same
way. I'd want my employees to kiss my customer's ass.
I can try really hard to pretend, but it's not my business.
If you care so much about your customer's ass, why
don't you kiss it? It's your business.

—*Gen Yer*

The general manager of a restaurant from a well-known chain
recently shared this story with me: "When he first came in for
his interview, this kid, let's call him Frank, told me, 'Oh yeah, I eat
here with my parents all the time.' Usually that's a good thing. If
you know what it's like to eat a meal here, you might have an idea
of what it's going to be like to work here. As soon as he started
working here, Frank's parents started coming in a lot more often,
and would often order something for Frank too, even though he was
working. They would come in, Frank would take their order, and
when his parents' order was up, he'd bring it to their table and sit
down to eat with them, sometimes for ten or fifteen minutes. I'd
walk by the table, and they'd all smile at me like there was nothing

weird about it at all. A few times Frank's mom invited me to sit down with them. She actually said to me, 'Isn't Frank just the greatest employee you've ever had? He's so busy with school and everything else. This is the only time we get to catch up with him. We have to pay to see our own son.' She actually said all that to me with a straight face," the manager continued.

"I explained to Frank that he couldn't just take a break in the middle of a shift to have dinner with his parents." What did Frank say to that? "He asked me why I spend so much time sitting with customers at their tables. So I explained that as the manager, I check on customers and sometimes sit down with my regular customers to make a personal connection. Frank says, 'Well, I'm bringing in customers here too. My parents are my number one customers. I'm just doing the same thing you do, making a personal connection with my regular customers.' Then he says, 'You know, I'm a regular customer of this place too. Maybe you should keep that in mind.'"

The restaurant manager explained that Frank wasn't just being difficult: "I think Frank was much more comfortable in the customer role. It's just that we don't pay our customers. They pay us. Frank really had a hard time transitioning out of that customer frame of mind and realizing he was in a different position when he was working here as an employee."

Gen Yer's Customer Mentality

Frank's story may be a little out of the ordinary, but the example is instructive because it highlights something our research points to over and over again, which is the strong customer mind-set of Generation Y. Gen Yers think like customers. Why? The marketplace has extended its reach beyond malls and into their homes through the Web. At the same time, because Gen Yers have had more buying power at a younger age than any other young generation in history, marketers have targeted them more aggressively than any new consumer market in history.

Once they reach school, don't Gen Yers think of themselves as students as opposed to customers? Yes and no. As the so-called customer service revolution has reached across the private and public sectors, institutions ranging from hospitals to universities have sought to incorporate the logic and practices of customer service into their standard operating procedures. Indeed, one professor at a small liberal arts college told me recently that the entire faculty of his institution was required to attend a customer service seminar led by an alumnus who is a retail entrepreneur. The goal of the seminar was to teach professors to treat everyone, students included, more like valued customers. Said the professor, "They want us to figure out the customers' needs and expectations, say 'please' and 'thank you' more often, and 'go the extra mile for our customers.' If I know my students, that means giving them very little homework and lots of A's. But that couldn't possibly be what the administration has in mind, could it?"

This may seem like the exception, but our research shows that this sort of thing is increasingly common, and apparently it's working. Here's what a Gen Yer had to say about his college experience: "I had one professor who missed three classes in the fall semester of my senior year. I figured out the lost value: three out of twenty-eight class sessions out of five classes I was taking. It was almost 3 percent of my semester tuition. I made up a bill and gave it to her and told her I wanted a refund for that much. She was pretty surprised and kind of laughed, I guess. I used to skip classes, of course. But I'm paying tuition, not the other way around."

Playing the customer or consumer role is usually Gen Yers' primary experience in the public sphere prior to arriving for their first day of work as employees. Many have little or no experience on the other side of the marketplace transaction, as vendors. "It carries over into their entire way of being," said a senior loan officer in a large financial services firm. "They come in the door with this expectant look on their face, like, 'Are you ready to give me a good job experience now? What's going to happen to me first? What is going to be done for me?'"

> Playing the customer or consumer role is usually Gen Yers' primary experience in the public sphere prior to arriving for their first day of work.

For their part, Gen Yers tell us they are ready to do their part, work hard, and do whatever is asked of them, within reason. They look at their own time, dedication, and best efforts as a kind of currency. They bring to the table their ability and willingness to work hard, and they want to know what they can buy with it. What kinds of success and rewards can they buy from your organization? What kinds of interesting experiences and conditions can they earn with their currency? They are on the edge of their seats, expectant indeed.

When You Are at Work, Everyone But You Is Your Customer

What's a manager to do? In our seminars, we teach managers to embrace and use Gen Yers' customer mind-set to give Gen Yers the basic context of the employment relationship. Explain: Employment is a transactional relationship, just like a customer relationship. This is the ultimate source of your employer's authority, plain and simple. This is the source of your obligations at work to everyone: your coworkers, your boss, your subordinates, and actual customers. The senior loan officer whose story I mentioned earlier takes this approach: "I tell them, 'You're not paying us. We're paying you. You are not the customer here. The company is. I am. You are on the other side of the transaction. When you are here at work, everyone else is the customer. Not you. Get it? Think about how you want to be treated, and treat everyone else that way. When you are at work, everyone is your customer.'"

"This is supposed to be the most entrepreneurial generation in history, right?" said one of the most successful entrepreneurs in the world. "They all think they want to be in business for themselves.

The funny thing is, they are already in business for themselves, whether they know it or not. They may be working for me, but how they present themselves, what kind of work they do—all that is going to have a bigger impact on their life and career than on me or my company. Who do they think they are representing when they come to work? Me? My company? Perhaps—if I let them anywhere near my customers. But mostly, they are representing themselves. What they need to understand is you've got to sell yourself, sell your services. What makes you valuable? What value are you adding right now? Why should someone pay you?"

Trumpet this message to your Gen Yers: Every person you deal with is your customer—coworkers, employees, managers, suppliers, service people, and actual customers. What makes you valuable to each customer? Every unmet need is an opportunity to add value. Deliver and go the extra mile; get it done early; add the bells and whistles, and tie a bow on it.

Gen Yers Spend a Lot of Time with Actual Customers

One of the best reasons to teach Gen Yers the basics of customer service is that they spend a lot of time dealing with actual customers. That's not just a Gen Y thing. That's a young worker thing. Young workers are disproportionately represented in frontline service roles because these roles are often the lower-tier positions. This is often the case in retail settings, but it's also true in many nonretail organizations too. In fact, most organizations seeking to scale their operations in any significant way will tend to put a young (and therefore relatively inexpensive) workforce out front.

"How do you know us?" asks the manager of a video store in a large chain. "You know us by the people behind the counter. The labor pool available for those jobs is usually pretty darned young. I can only hire who I can hire. But we get a lot of complaints about the younger counter help. Sometimes they are just unhelpful, distracted, doing their own thing, especially if the store is not too busy." We see this often in our research. I call the social dynamic that develops among frontline Gen Yers in a customer service environment the "cash register culture" of that workplace. Because they spend hour after hour with their coworkers, Gen Yers often care much more about attending to their relationships with their coworkers than their relationships with customers. Instead of the customer service mission, their relationships with each other become the context of the job for some Gen Yers.

One Gen Yer offered his perspective on this issue: "You have to understand. I'm here all day. We are here all day. This is my job. My coworkers are my friends, and we are hanging together all day. Customers are just passing through. They come in here, probably don't buy anything, or maybe they buy something. But they are just passing through. That's how I look at it. In a way, to be honest, it feels like they are interrupting my day."

Teach Gen Yers the Basics of Customer Service

In our customer service seminars, we teach six customer service best practices. Teach Gen Yers these six best practices.

1. Make Yourself Available

Being available doesn't necessarily require approaching customers, making eye contact, smiling, or extending verbal greetings, although this is the method many organizations favor. "Anybody who eats in restaurants has had the experience of trying to get their server's attention, and the server just won't look at you," said a senior executive in a large restaurant chain. He continued: "Avoiding that is what we're focused on. I don't need my servers to look guests in the eye, smile, introduce themselves, and spit out some corny line. That's what a lot of the competition is doing. I think some guests find that creepy. But if a guest is trying to catch your eye, you had better notice. If a guest is gesturing to you or trying to get your attention somehow, you had better notice. It's more about being visible, unobtrusive, and paying very close attention to your tables, even while you are running around."

2. Say as Little as Possible

The less you say, the less chance there is of saying something distracting, confusing, annoying, wrong, or even offensive. Saying less also saves time in any discussion and gives more air space to the customer. It's worth reminding Gen Yers that most people prefer to talk than to listen. So let the customer do most of the talking. Said the restaurant

> It's worth reminding Gen Yers that most people prefer to talk than to listen. So let the customer do most of the talking.

executive, "If you are going to listen carefully, that means you don't let your mind wander. You concentrate. You don't interrupt." One technique to let customers know you are really listening without saying very much is to take notes while they talk. But be prepared to show the customer those notes.

3. When You Do Talk, Choose Your Words Very Carefully

The safest words to say to a customer usually end in a question mark. Open-ended questions are a good place to start, such as, "Please will you tell me more about that?" Only when you think you really understand what the other person is saying, ask specific clarifying questions, such as, "Do you mean X?" or "Do I understand correctly that you are saying X?" Sometimes the most important words are the most basic: Always say "please" and "thank you." Never say, "I can't help you" or "no." Perhaps the best way to help Gen Yers to choose their words carefully is to help them choose their words in advance. Provide them with prepared materials, and encourage them to learn their lines and rehearse. "Our customers consistently rate our team members off the charts on customer service. That's our market differentiator," said the chief executive officer of a very successful high-end retail chain. How do they accomplish that? "Scripts. We treat customer service like a performance." The beauty of prepared materials is that they almost always provide a more thorough, precise, and attractive response than most frontline service personnel would otherwise offer on their own. These prepared materials also function as a training tool because Gen Yers usually learn some basic communication tactics that will serve them well anywhere they go.

4. Never Wing It

When it comes to saying words out loud to customers, don't guess, don't hope, and don't exaggerate. That means if it's going to be ten minutes, don't say, "That will be a couple of minutes." Rather, say, "That will be at least ten minutes." And sometimes the best thing to say is, "I don't know. Let me find out for you."

5. Request Feedback

Always confirm that the customer is happy and has no unsatisfied expectation or need at the moment. That can be accomplished by asking, "Is that acceptable?" Or "Are you happy with everything?" Or "Is there anything else you need?"

6. Problem-Solve

After identifying a problem, decide, "Do I have the knowledge, authority, and resources to solve this right here and now? Or do I need to find someone who does?" Once you learn what types of problems you should not try to solve on your own, you are much less likely to go beyond your discretion and exacerbate big problems that come to your attention. Once you've identified that a problem is outside your purview, gather basic information quickly and pass it to the right person as soon as possible. Then stay in the loop on these problems: How was the situation handled? What procedures were used? What information was needed to resolve it? Is that information readily available for future reference? That's how you turn this problem into one you can now handle on your own after all.

Convincing Gen Yers to Care About Customer Care

Of course, plenty of Gen Yers deliver acceptable, and even outstanding, customer service. But even in the best-case scenario, inevitably Gen Yers, just like any other employees, will make mistakes

> Never squander the teaching opportunities presented by customer service failures.

and fail to provide excellent customer service. Never squander the teaching opportunities presented by customer service failures. When these problems occur, it is your responsibility as the manager to intervene immediately and forcefully. Take time with all employees involved in a customer service failure and treat the instance as a crisis: Debrief those involved, identify the learning opportunities within, and review the steps that should have been taken.

Our research has identified the ten most common complaints about Gen Yers' delivery of customer service:

1. Gen Y service people are sometimes nowhere to be found.

2. They are sometimes present but they are not working; they are talking with each other or on the phone or otherwise unavailable.

3. They are sometimes available but are rude, rushed, or indifferent.

4. They are sometimes engaged and polite but unknowledgeable.

5. They sometimes provide customers with misinformation or conflicting information.

6. They are sometimes too slow.

7. They sometimes make mistakes.

8. They sometimes unnecessarily complicate transactions.

9. They are sometimes unable to solve small problems.

10. When customers do complain, they are sometimes unable to deal effectively with customer complaints.

Why do these complaints arise? Sometimes the front line is overstaffed—leading to a lack of urgency—or understaffed—leading to a lack of coverage. But usually the cause is that nobody has taught Gen Y employees the basics or convinced them to care about great customer service.

Sometimes Gen Yers don't realize that customer service is an extremely valuable skill that will make them more valuable in any role in any organization. "When I'm hiring, I always look for employees with real customer service experience," said a manager of underwriters in a large insurance company. "My people are highly analytical in their training, and their work requires them to be highly analytical. But they also have to deal with people. So finding someone who knows how to deal with people in a customer service job is a real plus to me." Customer service is a skill that does not become obsolete. Teach Gen Yers that every single customer service interaction is an opportunity to practice and fine-tune this valuable skill.

In our seminars, we teach managers to remind Gen Yers that providing good customer service has a huge impact on their ability to enjoy work—a huge concern for Gen Yers. Customers who feel ignored, underserved, or rebuffed by frontline service personnel tend to become frustrated and annoyed. These customers seek redress and create an uncomfortable atmosphere for all employees. "If a member has a miserable experience in the club, comes looking for me, and gives me a hard time, I'm going to look for the employee who's responsible and give that person a hard time," said the manager of a fitness club. "Keep the members happy, and we're all going to have a better day." In contrast, customers who feel well served tend to reflect their satisfaction, behave in a more relaxed manner, buy more, and express gratitude to service personnel.

We also teach managers to remind Gen Yers that investing effort in good service ultimately saves every employee a lot of time and energy, whereas bad customer service creates a downward spiral that makes everybody's job harder. "Unhappy customers cause a lot of problems that you don't see right away," said one assistant manager in a big box chain store. "They mess up store displays, move stuff around, spoil merchandise, buy less stuff." Unsatisfied customers are less respectful to employees and to the organization. When this downward spiral takes hold, employees spend a tremendous amount of time and energy soothing bad feelings, solving problems, and cleaning up the mess. If every frontline employee is focused on great service, unnecessary waste is kept to a minimum, and employees can use their valuable time and energy to build an upward spiral of success.

When it comes to selling your more ambitious Gen Yers on the importance of mastering customer service skills, emphasize that delivering great service is a valuable opportunity to network with customers. You don't want your employees handing out résumés to impressive-looking customers, but you should remind Gen Yers that every customer is a potential contact. Teach them not to make assumptions based on outward appearance, and make sure they know that every customer has the potential to help them in some way down the road.

"I was buying a home entertainment system and this young man was so good, so sharp, I was blown away. We walked out without buying, but this young man gave me his mobile and told me to phone with any questions. Later on when we went back to buy, he remembered us by name. When my wife was nervous about the installation, he offered to come to our home and supervise the installation. We took him up on that. In the end, I offered this young man a job working for me. That was years ago. Oh, he's made millions working for me."

We teach Gen Yers, regardless of age, size, shape, and attire, every customer has his or her own sphere of influence and authority. Every customer is worth impressing. Impressive people are impressed by those who are themselves positive, motivated, polite, focused on the task at hand, and go the extra mile. They will notice you. They will remember you. Learn their names, and they might learn yours.

> Emphasize that delivering great service is a valuable opportunity to network with customers.

Finally, you need to make sure that Gen Yers know that one way to get financial and nonfinancial rewards on your team is to deliver great service to customers. "You take care of our customers and I take care of you. That's how it works," said one manager. This means the best assignments, the best shifts, the best learning opportunities, exposure to decision makers, days off, cash, gift certificates, promotional giveaways, and everything else you have to offer should be reserved and allocated as rewards for customer service excellence. Reward those who succeed, and just as important, withhold rewards from those who fail. Use small rewards and use them frequently, and make sure you tie every reward directly to specific instances of performance.

CHAPTER SEVEN

TEACH THEM HOW TO MANAGE THEMSELVES

I know I am great. I don't need my boss to tell me I'm great. But I'm great at my talents, whereas you are probably great at your talents. We are both great in our own way. Me? I've always been the athlete who trains harder than anyone else, and that's who I am at work: the guy who will come in the earliest, stay the latest, do the heaviest lifting. But I'm not too good with details. I'll probably mess up on some of the details. Sorry. But I still know I'm great.

—*Gen Yer*

Here's a story a manager in a large research company told me: "The first time I interviewed this one employee, she told me, 'I think you are going to be really impressed.' Then when I hired her, she told me the same thing. The third time she repeated, 'I think you are going to be really impressed,' was on her first day of work. Well I was and I wasn't. She was very smart and she did high-quality work, in a whole other league than people with much more experience. But her work habits were horrendous. Where do I begin? She came in late, left early, took long breaks, and missed days of work. She lied about it too, always making excuses. She dressed inappropriately. She cursed a blue streak. She did great work, but very little of it. So I was impressed and then again I wasn't. In some ways she was superb. But she was just lacking in the basics."

Gen Yers are often amazingly advanced in their knowledge and skills at a very young age, yet they often lack maturity when it comes to the old-fashioned basics of productivity, quality, and behavior. What's worse, managers often report that Gen Yers tend to be unaware of gaps in these basic skills and are completely unconcerned about it. In response to this gap in skills, some managers just get frustrated. After all, when Gen Yers come to the workplace, shouldn't they already be mature enough to arrive on time, dress appropriately, practice good manners, stay focused on their key tasks, and do lots of work very well at a good, steady pace? Should managers be expected to teach them these sorts of things? As a restaurant manager put it, "Nobody taught *me* how to wipe *my* nose in my jobs. I had to learn how to manage myself."

That may be. But if you are the boss, then this gap in skills is your problem. If you manage Gen Yers who lack some of the basics of self-management, I'm sure you are frustrated too. Here's what you need to do: Help them. Lift them up. Make them better. Teach them to care about the basics. Teach them to be more aware of those gaps in their repertoires. Teach them to fill those gaps, one at a time. Teach them how to manage themselves.

Teach Them to Make the Most of Their Time

One of the paradoxes of Generation Y is that they are always in a hurry to get things done in the short term, but when it comes to longer-term goals, they often seem to lack a sense of urgency. "They don't realize how fleeting time is, how fast it goes," a senior executive in a major information systems company told me. But aren't Gen Yers plugged into today's fast pace even more than those of older generations? I asked. "That's true. They expect everything to be instant. They don't think in months or weeks; they think in hours and minutes. But they don't realize how little time there really is available to us. Every minute you spend on one thing is a minute you can't spend on something else. Some things take a long time to do, and if you don't do them right, sometimes they take even longer than they should. These young people spend way too much time on all the wrong things. They have to learn to spend their time more efficiently. It's about setting priorities."

Help Them Set Priorities

Setting priorities is usually step one in most time management programs and seminars. If you have limited time and too much to do, then you need to set priorities so that you control what gets done first, second, third, and so on in case you run out of time and have to leave some things unfinished. That setting priorities is the key to time management is obvious to most professionals. The hard part is teaching Gen Yers *how* to set priorities. According to that information systems company senior executive, "It's very hard to teach them how to set big-picture priorities because they don't have the big-picture information." He gave this example: "Most of our people work on multiple projects with different managers. When one of the senior managers pulls a programmer onto a project, he might be pulling the programmer off another project. Should that programmer—maybe a twenty-five-year-old kid with less than two years here—decide which is a priority? Should that programmer be put in that position? Of course not. How is he supposed to know that the project he's working on for a junior manager is actually more important to the company's big picture and should take priority over the project for the senior manager?"

When it comes to big-picture priorities, set clear priorities with Gen Yers, and communicate those priorities relentlessly. Make sure your Gen Yers are devoting the lion's share of their time to first and second priorities. When it comes to setting day-to-day priorities, teach Gen Yers how by setting priorities together with them. Let them know your thinking process. Walk through it with them: "This is first priority because X. This is second priority because Y. This is low priority because Z." Over time, you hope they learn. Until they learn, you have to keep making decisions for them or at least together with them. Teach Gen Yers to postpone low-priority activities until high-priority activities are well ahead of schedule. Those are the time windows during which lower-priority activities can be accomplished, starting with the top lower priorities, of course. Time wasters, on the other hand, should be eliminated altogether whenever possible.

Help Them Eliminate Time Wasters

Everyone has time wasters, but nobody can afford them, least of all people in the early stages of their careers who are eager to succeed but are also quite easily distracted. The best gift you can give Gen Yers is helping them to identify their big time wasters and eliminate them altogether. Probably the best tool for identifying time wasters is an old-fashioned time log or diary, in which an individual keeps track almost minute by minute of what she is doing. The idea is that each time the person changes from one activity to another, she notes briefly the time and the activity. Here's an example:

8:00 A.M.	Sat down at my desk, turned on computer
8:10 A.M.	Got up to use bathroom and get coffee
9:15 A.M.	Sat back down at desk, opened e-mail.
9:30 A.M.	Started preparing response to e-mail from Client Jones
9:40 A.M.	Incoming phone call from Friend Smith
10:15 A.M.	Continued preparing response to e-mail from Client Jones
10:25 A.M.	Got up to use bathroom and get another cup of coffee

The time log is useful only if the user faithfully logs every activity precisely. Used properly, three or four days is all it takes to get a reality check on how a person is spending her time. How much time is spent on first, second, or third priorities? What are the big time wasters that can be eliminated to free up time?

Remember that Gen Yers treasure time above all other non-financial rewards. When you help them eliminate time wasters and limit the time they spend on low priorities, you are helping them focus their time on top priorities and giving them free time they otherwise would have wasted. That is a reward that keeps on giving. They'll really appreciate it.

> The best gift you can give Gen Yers is helping them to identify their big time wasters and eliminate them altogether.

When helping Gen Yers identify time wasters to eliminate, don't mistake distractions for time wasters. They may or not be. Remember that Gen Yers are used to multitasking—they've been doing their homework for years with an MP3 player in one ear and a cell phone buzzing text messages on the table. Just because it might be distracting to you doesn't mean it is distracting to them. If the task in question is being performed well within expected time frames, then the employee is probably not distracted. Pay attention to which of the so-called distractions help them remain absorbed in their tasks at work as opposed to those that draw their attention away.

Teach Them How to Live by a Schedule

"For people who are supposed to be in a hurry all the time, Gen Yers sure take their time getting to work. They are the worst offenders bar none when it comes to tardiness," said a manager in a medical laboratory. She continued, "They take their time getting through their work too. Deadlines mean little to them. They just say, 'Oh, yeah, sorry it's late.' I say, 'That's not okay,' and they say, 'Yeah, I'm really sorry.' Then it's late the next time too. Most of them do a great job. They're just always late doing it."

Tardiness, whether it is coming late to work or missing deadlines, is one of managers' top complaints about Gen Yers. And while managers often attribute Gen Yers' tardiness to a blasé attitude and a lack of care, consideration, or diligence, our research shows that Gen Yers' tardiness is almost always due to a lack of good planning. When it comes to planning time, there is really no better tool than a good old-fashioned schedule. Once again, you have to teach them the basics.

Here's why. On one hand, what Gen Yers really want, when it comes to time management, is greater freedom. On the other hand, they grew up as the most overscheduled generation in history, so they actually like schedules. The problem is that Gen Yers are used to schedules customized to their particular life circumstances, needs, and wants. One Gen Yer told me, "I've been working here for four months, and their early morning schedule is hard for me. I'm used to staying up all night writing papers and studying for exams. If you had to skip a class or show up to class late because you've been up all night studying, nobody was going to chew your head off. If you needed an extension on a paper, you could get one. Once I had an exam rescheduled because I wasn't ready."

Ultimately Gen Yers want more flexibility about when they work, more control over their time while they are working, and more free time outside work. Thus, in order to get what they want, they need a lot of help getting lots of work done very well, very fast while they are at work. The trick to doing that is teaching them how to use a schedule to better plan their hours, minutes, and seconds around their priorities—inside and outside work.

A smart retail manager told me this story about using schedules to help a Gen Yer get to work on time: "When I have people who are chronically late, I've learned that usually they need help being on time. I just had this experience with a young employee, Paul. Paul was always on time for the evening shift but always late for the morning shift. At first I thought he was trying to get me to give him the late shift every week. But when I talked to him, I found out that he had never really tuned in to the fact that it took him longer to get ready and get to work in the morning than in the afternoon. I mean, he knew it in the back of his head, but he had never really taken it into account."

The retail manager continued, "I had to help Paul learn how to be on time. So I took out a piece of paper and we wrote a schedule, working backward from 8:00 A.M.: 'Walk in the front door at work at 7:55 A.M. Leave Dunkin' Donuts parking lot by 7:35 A.M. Pull in to Dunkin' Donuts parking lot by 7:25 A.M. Leave home by 7:10 A.M.

Get back from walking dog by 7:00 A.M.'" Is it appropriate to help an employee plan out details as personal as what time he will walk his dog?

No matter how rigorously employees schedule their work time, if they can't manage their nonwork time, they often come late to work, leave early, call in sick, spend work time doing nonwork activities, and so on. I asked the retail manager how this approach worked with Paul. "I was afraid he would be insulted, but the look on his face was pure gratitude. He was saying, 'That really helps me, that really helps me.' Not only has he been chronically on time ever since we did the schedule, but now he counts out everything backward in his day planner. I offered to get him a PDA as a reward for doing so great, but he said 'no thanks.' He is attached to that little day planner. Those are habits that really stuck for him." Hooray for Paul! Hooray for this manager!!

Most Gen Yers report they have more to do at work than they can fit into their work schedule and more they want to do outside work than they can do in their limited free time. Many are chronically overtired and seriously overscheduled. One Gen Yer told me: "I don't stay past five or six at work because I don't have time to stay. There is the dance class I am taking, the dance class I am teaching, and all these new friends and my old friends. I'm up until 3 A.M., and then I'm at my desk by 9 A.M., Monday through Saturday. It's not like I'm not working. I'm so busy all day at work, I don't have any time left to be in the game."

When teaching Gen Yers how to manage their schedule, you need to start somewhere. Sleeping is where I always start. Tell them to block 56 hours every week for sleeping, ideally in 8-hour increments. Block another hour a day for downtime, ideally around the sleep time. That leaves them with 105 hours to be awake and "in the game" each week. Then what? If they don't plan their nonwork time leading up to the time they walk in the door at work, there is a good chance they'll be late for work. If they don't plan their nonwork time after work, there is a good chance they'll be late the next day or else be stressed and distracted.

The only way to harmonize work time and nonwork time is to keep *one* schedule. Teach them this basic fact of life and they will probably be very grateful.

Teach Them How to Make a Plan

Schedules are useful tools only if they reflect accurate planning. Often what looks like a perfectly good schedule turns out to be a fantasy—a wishful projection for how we might spend our very limited time.

Here's a story told to me by the manager of a new Gen Y employee in a massive international consumer products company: "Greg, an ambitious young man, was missing deadlines from the get-go on his first project. I was thrown off because when he started the project, he had impressed me with a plan very carefully broken out into short-term goals with short-term deadlines along the way." When the manager sat down with Greg to talk about the missed deadlines, they both realized that the initial schedule Greg had drafted was based on unrealistic time lines. "They were all just guesses. Uneducated guesses at that. The big lesson for Greg was that timetables are no good if you don't figure out how long each goal is actually going to take to complete. " After their conversation, the manager explained, "Greg was able to make new timetables and meet every one of those very realistic new short-term deadlines."

Before you can make a realistic plan, you have to know how long each task is actually going to take. That sounds obvious, but we've seen over and over again in our research that Gen Yers miss deadlines because they are missing this basic step. "The big lesson for me," said the manager at the consumer products company, "was that you really have to teach them how to make a plan. Greg knew enough to take a big project and break it down into a timetable, and he knew enough to make a plan. But he just didn't know *how* to make a plan."

Teach them how. Teach them how to start with a big project, break it into manageable tasks, estimate accurately how long it will take them to complete each of the tasks, and then set a timetable of short-term deadlines based on those realistic estimates.

Sometimes Gen Yers resist planning because they are so certain that things will change anyway. In an uncertain world, what's the point in planning? It's worth explaining to them that one of the hidden benefits of plans and schedules is that they

> Teach Gen Yers not to be thrown off when real-life interruptions veer them off course from their well-made plans.

can be used by managers to provide employees with more flexibility while still strictly enforcing deadlines. But also let Gen Yers know you understand that no matter how great the plan, plans are always subject to real-life interruptions. Emergencies, wild-goose chases, and distractions often spring up and disrupt the progress of a perfectly realistic plan. Teach Gen Yers not to be thrown off when real-life interruptions veer them off course from their well-made plans. Teach them to pay close attention to real life and be prepared to revise and adjust their plans every step of the way.

Teach Them to Take Notes and Use Checklists

A young employee recently shared this story with me: "There's a lot to keep track of at work. It would help me a lot if they would give me step-by-step instructions. I mean, whose job is it to make sure we do our jobs right? I'm trying pretty hard, but you don't get an A for effort around here. Sometimes I'll ask them, 'Could you give me instructions so I don't waste a bunch of my time?' You'd think they'd like that, but they say, 'Look, I can't do your job for you. I shouldn't have to tell you how to do your job.' That makes no sense. How am I supposed to do my job if you don't tell me how?"

This Gen Yer is right. It's not enough to teach Gen Yers to use schedules and make plans. You should also teach them to take notes and use checklists to get their jobs done properly. Managers often complain that Gen Yers are full of energy and gumption, but they have a hard time focusing that energy on the work that needs to get done. Managers report that even when Gen Yers do high-quality work in a timely manner, they often overlook important details or leave out important pieces of otherwise finished results. Our research shows that when managers require Gen Yers to take notes and make rigorous use of checklists, their error rates go down, quality goes up, and assignments are more likely to be completed in their entirety.

Teach Them to Take Notes

"In one ear and out the other," said a construction supervisor in a major real estate development company. "I would say to this one guy over and over again, 'The details really matter.' He was nodding his head, but I couldn't tell if he was nodding to me or nodding with the music he was listening to. So finally I started making him take notes whenever I talked to him. Since he didn't have anything to write with but I noticed he was always on his cell phone texting, I told him, 'Send yourself a text message.' He focused on me like he never had before, texting into his phone the gist of what I was saying. Finally I said, 'Send me a copy of that,' and that's how that started. Now he takes notes on his cell phone and sends a copy to me and to him. I print them out and I'll go back to him the next day, with his text message in hand, and it serves as a great reference. He usually grabs that sheet of paper, gives it a look-over, and tucks it in his back pocket. I see him checking it later as he's going about his business. I think it helps him focus. Sometimes I take his text message and turn it into a checklist to use with all the guys. Checklists help them focus."

Checklists are very common in workplaces where there is little room for error: operating rooms, airplane cockpits, nuclear weapons launch sites, accounting firms, and so on. Of course, checklists are useful only if they are used.

Help Them Use Checklists

A lead flight attendant for a major airline gave me this example: "The younger crew members are not lazy. I left the preflight safety demonstration to one attendant because she had been rehearsing it so much and she really wanted to practice it live. I think she had been with us for only a few weeks. When she did the demonstration, she practically sang it. Passengers looked up and listened, which is pretty unusual. But she forgot to do electronic devices. While we were taking off, I realized there were passengers still on the phone and working on computers and a kid playing a video game. These are huge FAA violations. We have procedures and checklists, of course, but if the person in charge isn't really making sure people use them, then they don't actually serve their purpose."

Here's another example, provided by a senior manager in a major accounting firm: "We are an accounting firm, so we have to use checklists. Even with all of our checklists, the less experienced staff will hand in work product that's not complete. Sometimes they know it's not complete. They'll even attach a note saying, for example, 'Section 4b is missing key pieces of information and section 5c is blank. Please complete,' like I am supposed to finish their work for them. Other times they don't even know it's not complete. I'm not sure which is worse. Either way, about half the time, I would find myself finishing up work for them before it could actually be submitted. I called it 'delegating the work back up.'"

Our research shows that turning in incomplete work is a common complaint about Gen Yers. What is the solution? Managers in these cases need to treat the delivery of incomplete work as an intermediate step, just another teachable moment, and another chance to get them back to the basics of self-management. Sometimes you need to teach them how to finish a product.

"When they try delegating work back up to me now, I will go over the checklist with them. Section 4b is not done until you have every piece of information. Section 5 is not done if section 5c is blank. That's when you have to make a checklist for the checklist. Sometimes they need a checklist for the checklist for the checklist."

Teach Gen Yers to take notes. And teach them to turn their notes into checklists to guide them. If you already have checklists, teach Gen Yers to follow checklists as step-by-step instructions to help them ensure quality and completeness in their work. If necessary, help them make checklists for the checklists. But remember the real trick is teaching them to actually use the checklist. Sometimes you have to remind them that the reason it's called a "checklist" is because, as you complete each item, you need to take a pen and go "check."

Teach Them the Values of Good Workplace Citizenship

One Gen Yer shared this with me: "Somebody told me if you are idealistic when you are old, you are stupid, but if you are cynical when you are still young, then you just suck. I'm definitely idealistic, but I guess I kind of suck too, because I'm also kind of cynical already."

Indeed, idealism is a privilege and burden of youth. But Gen Yers' idealism may look very different from that of generations past. All the leading research shows that Gen Yers are more idealistic than any other new youth cohort since the first wave of baby boomers came of age in the 1960s. Gen Yers are more concerned about the well-being of the planet, humankind, and their communities than most older cohorts were in their twenties. Most Gen Yers say there are causes and values they believe in enough that they would be willing to sacrifice their own time, money, comfort, and even well-being. They often look to values issues when they are considering a new job: Do they believe in the company's mission? Do they approve of how you do business? This, I believe, is good news.

What is often confusing to managers is that they have a hard time pinning down Gen Yers on the values spectrum in a way they can understand. "When I'm hiring young entry-level employees, I'm looking for a good values fit," said a senior executive in a leading energy services company. "With this generation, it seems like anything goes, more or less. No respect for tradition, no respect for their elders, no respect for experience, no respect

> Gen Yers often look to values issues when they are considering a new job. This, I believe, is good news.

for all the old-fashioned values: discretion, diligence, courtesy, honesty. You pick the clean-cut kid with Eagle Scout on his résumé, and he shows up late to work, bad-mouths his coworkers, and steals the stapler off your desk. Then you look at this long-haired kid who is listening to music on his MP3 player all day and he shows up to work early, works hard, stays late, says 'yes sir' and 'yes ma'am' and 'please' and 'thank you.' It used to be that I could pick them out of a crowd. Not anymore. Not with this generation. How do you find the Good ones? I mean the capital G good ones."

Managers tell us every day that they have a hard time understanding how Gen Yers look at traditional values issues. Are they the new idealists portrayed by some observers, or are they the post-values generation for whom anything goes? Over and over again, we find that Gen Yers' ideals tend to be rather idiosyncratic. They are products of an information environment that allows them to mix and match seemingly unrelated or incompatible beliefs. Like everything else in their lives, Gen Yers customize their deep inner values. For example, it is not uncommon to find a Gen Yer who considers himself a person of faith, but not one you would likely recognize. This Gen Yer explained, "I was born and raised Baptist, and I am still Baptist. I go to church sometimes with my parents to supercharge my spirit. But mostly I'm into Buddhist teachings right now. To me there is nothing inconsistent about that. It's my own religion, I guess."

Given this inscrutable nature, how can managers identify Gen Yers who are more likely to manifest those good old-fashioned values the senior executive was talking about above: discretion, diligence, courtesy, and honesty? As he put it, "How do you find the good ones?"

Our research shows that you can't and you shouldn't even try. You simply cannot divine deep inner values from interviews, tests, recommendations, and résumés. In fact, trying to figure out who Gen Yers are deep inside is the wrong tactic. How can you possibly figure out what their mind and spirit are really like? How can you figure out what their inner motivations really are? You are not qualified to do so. And I would argue that it's really none of your business anyway.

"So, can you teach them traditional values?" the senior executive asked me. Here's what we've learned. You cannot—and should not—teach them what to believe, but you can certainly teach them how to behave. It's not really your place to teach them values. But it is certainly your place to teach them how to be good citizens within your organization. Where do you start?

Define What It Means to Be a Good Citizen in Your Company

The CEO of a small software company I've worked with gained some notoriety a few years back with his "no-jerks" policy. What did that mean exactly? According to one manager who worked for that CEO, "It was a little vague, but it was meant to capture those intangibles like your attitude, how you talk to people, how you treat people. Not exactly what kind of person are you, but how you conduct yourself with colleagues, with customers, with vendors. When something comes up, do you try to blame other people? Are you saying nasty things behind other people's backs? Do you make excuses? Are you cutting out when everybody else is busting their humps staying all night?" Is a no-jerks policy really so much more vague than encouraging people to practice discretion, diligence, courtesy, and honesty? Maybe a little bit. But these values mean different things to different people. That's why they can be so hard to teach. Still, such intangible elements of performance often matter a lot to managers and have a big impact on an employee's ability to succeed in a particular organization.

What does it really mean to be a good citizen in your workplace? The key is to create shared meaning through shared language and experience. In the military, enlisted people are taught to salute and call officers sir and ma'am. One trend on the rise in the workplace is etiquette training, in which young employees are taught good old-fashioned manners, like saying please and thank you. Safeway caused a stir back in the late 1990s when they asked store employees to make eye contact with customers and smile. It was controversial, but at least the requirement was clear.

Decide what really matters in your organization, and keep it simple. Whatever values you want them to practice, you have to do the hard work of making the intangible more tangible. What do discretion, diligence, courtesy, and honesty actually look like in your workplace? Describe it. Spell it out and break it down for them.

But one word of caution: Gen Yers have giant BS detectors. If you want to teach them about good workplace citizenship, you had better not act like a jerk. As the manager I mentioned earlier said, the "no-jerk" policy "put a lot of pressure on those of us in the leadership team to not act like jerks, which was good I think. Everyone has their moments, and you would definitely hear about it from some of the younger folks who don't really hold back. You'd get this, 'Who's acting like a jerk now?' So you definitely had to walk the talk."

You Can't Teach Good Judgment, But You Can Teach the Habits of Critical Thinking

Managers often tell us that one of the biggest constraints on maximizing young workers is their lack of seasoned judgment.

What is good judgment anyway? It's not the same thing as natural intelligence. It's not a matter of accumulated knowledge or memorized information. It is more than the mastery of techniques and tools. In very simple terms, good judgment is the ability to see the connection between causes and their effects. Going forward, good judgment allows one to project likely outcomes—to accurately predict the consequences of specific decisions and actions. In retrospect, good judgment allows one to work backward from effects to assess likely causes, to figure out what decisions and actions led to the current situation.

One senior executive in a large media company said: "Good judgment. That's the ultimate. I don't want my young employees to improvise most of the time. I want them to

> One senior executive in a large media company said: "Good judgment. That's the ultimate."

follow our established procedures. But we don't have procedures for everything. I can try hard to anticipate situations they are likely to encounter and help them prepare for those situations. But I can't anticipate every possible situation. There are times when they just have to use good judgment. But they are just too young and don't have enough experience to have good judgment.

Putting aside those rare people who are wise beyond their years, are age and experience prerequisites for good judgment? The answer is, in part, yes. Experience means participating—feeling, tasting, hearing, seeing, smelling—in the unfolding of life events. Life events unfold over time. By definition, the more time passes, the more experience one has. That's why experience and age often lead to improved judgment. Of course, you can't fast-forward time or wait for your Gen Y employees to grow older and acquire judgment. So how can you improve their judgment?

Expose Them to New Experiences

One factor in determining good judgment is the quality of a person's experiences. Are his experiences diverse or monotonous? Deep or glancing? Has he experienced richly many different kinds of causes and been able to observe their various effects? This is the logic behind rotation programs in which employees are given a series of relatively short-term assignments (usually a matter of months) in different types of operations in different parts of the company, sometimes in different parts of the world. The idea is exposure, plain and simple.

If you have the resources, give Gen Yers more experience faster by putting them on rotation programs. Even with limited resources, you can give them more experience through more diverse and deep exposure. Move them around to different parts of your company once in a while, even if that means the other side of the building. Let them try out different tasks, responsibilities, and projects. Encourage them to interact with different employees, vendors, and customers.

Teach Them to Be Strategic

The single most important factor in good judgment is how a person thinks about her life experiences. Does she think about cause and effect? Does she stop and reflect before making decisions and taking actions? Does she project likely outcomes in advance? Does she look at each decision and action as a set of choices, each with identifiable consequences?

If you've played chess or any other game of strategy, you know what I mean. The key to success is thinking ahead. Before making a move, you play out in your head the likely outcomes, often over a long sequence of moves and countermoves. If I do A, the other player would probably respond with B. Then I would do C, and he would probably respond with D. Then I would do E, and he would probably respond with F. And so on. This is what strategic planners call a decision/action tree because each decision or action is the beginning of a branch of responses and counterresponses. In fact, each decision or action creates a series of possible responses, and each possible response creates a series of possible counterresponses.

Teach Gen Yers to be strategic by using decision/action trees every step of the way. Teach them to think ahead and play out the likely sequence of moves and countermoves before making a move: "If you take this decision or action, who is likely to respond, how, when, where, and why? What set of options will this create? What set of options will this cut off? How will it play out if you take this other decision/action instead?"

Teach Them to Look at Past Experiences— Their Own and Others'

That media company senior executive asked me, "How does a person learn real-life lessons faster than he can experience real life? Is there any way to jump-start this process?" One way is to learn from the life experiences of others or from history. This is why the case study method is used by most business schools. Real company cases are presented to students in detail. Who were the key players? What were their interests and objectives? What happened? How did it happen? Where? When? What were the outcomes? Students are then taught to apply the methods of critical thinking to the facts of the case. They are taught to suspend judgment, question assumptions, uncover the facts, and then rigorously analyze the decisions and actions taken by different key players in the case study. The pedagogy is simple: Look at the outcomes and trace them back to see the chains of cause and effect.

You can jump-start their learning by giving Gen Yers a little taste of business school in real life. Give them real cases to study, and teach them to use the case study method. Teach them to apply the methods of critical thinking to the real-life experiences of others. Give them a simple one-page worksheet (see facing page) to analyze real cases.

Maybe the most important thing you can do to jump-start Gen Yers' development of good judgment is teaching them to scrutinize their own experiences during and after they actually occur. Teach them to stop and reflect after making decisions and taking actions. Teach them to stop and reflect on outcomes and consequences. This is the essence of the lessons-learned process that is ubiquitous in the military and intelligence agencies. Every mission is subjected to intense scrutiny immediately after the fact. Leaders at all levels involved in a mission are expected to go over every decision and action, step by step, to determine exactly what happened and why. Then they meet to discuss and debate these decisions and actions. As one U.S. Army officer told me, "It is our duty to second-guess and third-guess and fourth-guess and fifth-guess every move we make." Lessons learned from real experience are meant to guide the planning and execution of future missions. Said the Army officer, "We are at war, so we use lessons learned the next day or the same day sometimes. This is real time learning in action."

Teach Gen Yers to apply the lessons-learned process to every "mission" they undertake, to every move they make. Ask them to subject their decisions and actions to much greater scrutiny every step of the way: What were the specific causes of each outcome or

What actually happened, step by step?

WHEN   WHO   WHAT   WHERE   HOW   WHY

_____

_____

_____

What decisions were made? Who made them? Why? What was the outcome?

DECISIONS   WHO?   WHY?   OUTCOME

_____

_____

_____

What actions were taken? Who made them? Why? What was the outcome?

ACTIONS   WHO?   WHY?   OUTCOME

_____

_____

_____

What were the leading alternative decisions that were not made? What different outcomes might have occurred?

ALTERNATIVE DECISIONS   POSSIBLE DIFFERENT OUTCOMES

_____   _____

_____   _____

_____   _____

What were the leading alternative actions that were not taken? What different outcomes might have occurred?

ALTERNATIVE ACTIONS   POSSIBLE DIFFERENT OUTCOMES

_____   _____

_____   _____

_____   _____

consequence? Consider giving them this one-page worksheet to help them analyze their own decisions and actions.

Self-Evaluation Is the Beginning, Middle, and End of Self-Management

Rigorous self-evaluation is not just a key component of learning good judgment. It is the beginning, middle, and end of self-management. It is the essential habit of self-improvement. If you teach Gen Yers one thing, teach them to make a commitment to constant, rigorous self-evaluation. Teach them to assess their use of time, the productivity and quality of their work, and their behavior. Teach them to ask themselves these questions:

Productivity: Am I getting enough work done fast enough? What can I do to get more work done faster? Should I revisit my priorities? Do I need to focus my time better? Do I need to postpone low-priority activities? How can I eliminate time wasters? Do I need better time budgets? Do I need to make better plans?

Quality: Am I meeting or exceeding guidelines and specifications for my tasks and responsibilities? What can I do to improve my work? Do I need to make better use of checklists? Do I need to start adding some bells and whistles to my work product?

Behavior: What can I do to be a better workplace citizen? Are there substandard behaviors I can eliminate? Are there superstar behaviors I can start adding? Should I be taking more initiative or less? How can I take more initiative without overstepping my bounds?

Of course, self-evaluation is an engine of self-improvement only if you use the information you've learned from it. So teach them to focus on their self-evaluation and really use what they learn from it. Teach them to start on one little goal at a time—the smaller the better. For example, if someone wants to become a better workplace citizen, that's a pretty big bite to chew on. Carve it up. Encourage him to start with something simple such as: "Step one, stop swearing. Practice saying *dagnabbit* and *gee whiz* instead of curse words." Once he has met that goal, encourage him to take on another small bite: "Step two, stop bad-mouthing your colleagues. Practice biting your tongue when you feel the urge to say something nasty. Practice saying nice things about people."

> If you teach Gen Yers one thing, teach them to make a commitment to constant, rigorous self-evaluation.

And always remind them that self-management and self-improvement come one small step at a time. It's a never-ending process because there is always room to improve.

CHAPTER EIGHT

TEACH THEM HOW TO BE MANAGED BY YOU

> When I start working with a new boss, it's like taking a new class. You know, the first day of class they say, "Here's what this class is about. Here are my rules: You can miss three classes before it affects your grade, there will be three quizzes, a term paper, and an exam." I've had bosses who do that and I think it really helps a lot.
>
> —Gen Yer

Some people know how to be managed and others just don't," said a senior partner at a major American law firm whom I'll call Mr. Rust. "I can tell almost immediately with a new associate if I'm going to be able to work with that person and if that person is going to be able to work with me. Some of the young associates today still come in with a good work ethic, good work habits; the kind of work style I can mesh with. Most of them don't."

I hear this from a lot of leaders and managers. They claim that many Gen Yers are lacking when it comes to work ethic, work habits, and work style. The underlying truth of this common complaint is that work ethic, habits, and style are often less developed in younger workers. But it's a mistake to assume that young employees will just grow up and take on old-fashioned attitudes and behavior that older generations exhibit. You simply cannot ignore the impact of Gen Yers' short-term transactional approach to work and their insistence on customizing the details of their working lives to optimize their needs and wants.

These factors leave a lot of managers baffled and looking for the exceptions in the young talent pool—those young employees who seem to manifest a more traditional approach to work and already know how to be managed. Such leaders and managers assume that some young employees have it—the good work ethic, habits, and style—while others simply do not. But often what these leaders are really looking for, whether they realize it or not, is an employee whose own work ethic, habits, and style are a good match with theirs. Often when leaders reject new employees, it's because they perceive a bad match. They act as if these were matters set in stone.

When I pressed Mr. Rust, the senior partner at the law firm, he allowed that "some of the associates who seem like losers to me go on to work just fine with one of the other partners. Talk to my partner Mr. Gold. Gold makes lemonade out of lemons. Gold can work with any of these young associates. They all love Gold."

Mr. Gold sounded like someone I wanted to know.

Here's what Mr. Gold had to say, "Rust is a great lawyer and a great guy, but he's very finicky about how things are done. He's got standards that are very much his own. I would have a hard time working for him. Rust has some very interesting work, though, so a lot of the new associates want to work for him, at least when they first get here." Then Mr. Gold told me a great story about a young associate who came to their firm determined to work with Mr. Rust, despite his reputation for being finicky. This young associate, Mr. Gold told me, "had been here for a summer in law school and he was very clever. When he came back as an associate, his first day here, he went and made appointments with the three senior associates who work with Rust. He sat down with them, one by one, and interviewed them and took extensive notes, 'What time does Rust get to the office? What time does he leave? What time does he have lunch?

Does he respond to e-mail? Does he like memos double-spaced?' Then, presto! He's one of the associates who can work with Rust!"

Wasn't that young associate just doing his job well by figuring out how to fit with Mr. Rust's work ethic, habits, and style? I asked Mr. Gold. After all, if he wants to work for Mr. Rust, he should take the initiative and figure out how to work for Mr. Rust. "That's just it," said Mr. Gold. "Most of the associates don't take the initiative. They don't figure it out."

Since Mr. Gold had a reputation for working well with the young associates, I asked him what his secret was. "What that young associate did with Rust, I do with every associate. I take that initiative for them. I make it so they don't have to be so clever." Mr. Gold continued, "I tell them, 'This is who I am. This is what I work on. This is what time I come in. This is what time I usually leave. This is what I expect from you. This is how to work for me.'" I asked Mr. Gold if he agreed with Mr. Rust that "some people know how to be managed and others don't." Mr. Gold said, "It's actually, 'Does this person know how to be managed by *you*?' I guess the difference is that I see teaching them how to be managed by me as my responsibility. I'm not going to teach them how to be managed by Rust. But I can teach them how to be managed by me. You have to tell them, 'It's not you, it's me,'" said Mr. Gold. "That's a good place to start."

Set Clear Ground Rules Up Front

Managers tell me every day that Gen Yers fail to meet a lot of unspoken expectations about behavior in the workplace. I have an idea: Speak them!

One credit union manager was telling me about a young employee who routinely came to work late and then made lots of personal calls on his cell phone throughout the workday. "Do I really need to tell him, 'Come to work on time, and it's not good to make so many personal calls all day long'?" Yes! You have to tell him, up front and every step of the way.

"I would make lots of offhand comments to him like, 'Hey, you know, trickle in here whenever you feel like it. Don't feel any pressure to come to work on time. Make all the calls you want.' But he just wasn't getting the hint." The manager continued, "At the end of my rope, I pulled this guy aside. I had worried so much about having the conversation, worried it was going to be a big blow-up. When I said to him, 'It's really not acceptable to come to work late,' he said, 'Really? Why didn't you just say so?' When I told him, 'You really are only supposed to make personal calls on your cell phone at a break or at lunch or in the case of an emergency,' he said, 'Really? Why didn't you just say so?' Then he went into this whole spiel: 'What else aren't you tellin' me, Sparky? Sparky, you gotta tell me stuff that's important to ya.' So I told him, 'There is one other thing. Please stop calling me Sparky. You can call me Rob, or you can call me Mr. Sarkington.'"

Gen Yers will be open and direct with you if you give them the chance. One Gen Yer recently told me, "My boss never gets to the point. You don't have to give me a whole line of BS. Don't even try to sweeten it up for me. I can just take it. Just be real. Just get to the point." Indeed, being open with Gen Yers will help you keep tabs on their attitude, behavior, shifting loyalties, and commitments in and out of the workplace. The problem is that in an effort to foster that openness, some managers find themselves getting dragged into time-consuming and uncomfortable personal territory that really should be avoided. The other problem is that in order to avoid personal minefields, managers often end up soft-pedaling their requirements and withholding candid feedback no matter how fair and straightforward it might be.

Set Ground Rules on the Intangibles

"This young woman who worked in our office was always coming in moping around here," I was told by a manager in a medical devices company. "She always had an excuse. Her personal life was always out there. Bad days for her were bad days for everyone. Ironically, if you tried to talk to her about the fact that she was leaving early or moping around, she'd freeze right up. Even if I tried to say, 'I know you locked your keys in the car, I know you had to go to Cleveland, I know your uncle is sick, but you really can't leave until your shift is over,' she'd turn around and tell me in this cold, harsh tone, 'My personal life is none of your business.'" The manager continued, "I finally sat down with her and said, 'Listen, it's up to you whether or not you want to share your personal issues with people here at work. But you need to do that outside your work time.' I told her, 'Your personal life is your own business, but you can't let your personal issues interfere with our business here. You have to follow the same ground rules as everybody else.'"

The manager continued, "When she started to freeze up, I told her, 'You can't freeze up now. We have to be able to talk about your job performance. This isn't about your personal life. You can't use your personal life as an excuse for leaving early and then the next day tell me it's none of my business.' You need to leave your personal issues at the door when you come to work. This is a place where you focus on work. You don't need to feel bad about your personal problems here. You can feel good about your work. But you have to smile. Use a pleasant tone of voice. Fake it if you have to. When you come in here, you have to be professional.' To my total delight and surprise, she was fine after that—not that she didn't slip up now and then. My catch-phrase with her after that was, 'Fake it if you have to.' That was my way of reminding her to be professional. I told her, 'I have to be able to talk to you about your performance without you freezing up. I have to be able to tell you when your performance is lagging and you need to improve. We have to be able to have these conversations.'"

> You may need to say, "Whenever you are working with me, on any task, for any period of time, these are MY ground rules."

I hear success stories like this every day from smart managers who are willing to put it on the line and take charge. You have to figure out what your expectations are and then speak up. Set ground rules. Maybe there are corporate policies in place already. But often there are no concrete policies to regulate important intangibles like attitude, tone of voice, and other subtleties of professionalism in the workplace. You may need to figure out these ground rules on your own. You may need to say, "Whenever you are working with me, on any task, for any period of time, these are MY ground rules." Then lay out your ground rules in no uncertain terms, and make it clear they are deal breakers for *you*. Explain that you can't work with someone who doesn't follow these ground rules.

Set Ground Rules That Matter

One word of caution: Don't set too many ground rules, or the ground rules will lose meaning. Also, don't set ground rules just because they are your pet peeves, or they will have no legitimacy. Be honest and rigorous with yourself. What is the business logic behind each ground rule? What do you lose or risk losing as a result of this ground rule? What do you gain? Is it worth it?

Ground rules will be your fundamental performance requirements, so take some time to brainstorm about the broad standards that really matter: Attire? Attitude? Conduct? Cursing? Personal issues? Personal calls? Personal business on company time? What about work hours? Will we keep our conversations focused on work? When I give you directions, can I expect you to ask clarifying questions? Can I ask you to spell out for me the steps you are going to take to execute my instructions? Can I expect you to write things down?

The more you spell out clear ground rules up front, the better things will go. Make your ground rules clear. Use catch-phrases if they come naturally. Then speak them. Write them down. And speak them some more. They will serve as an easy point of reference whenever you want to remind an employee, "We both know that this is one of my ground rules."

Establish a Regular Time
and Place for One-on-Ones

Remember that Gen Yers have grown up hyperscheduled. They thrive on that kind of structure, and they thrive on one-on-one attention. One of the most effective ways to help your young employees learn to be managed by you is to schedule regular discussions with each of them about their work.

At first, err on the side of meeting more often with each person—every day, every other day, or once a week. Start by evaluating what time will best work for you: What time will fit your regular schedule and needs? Also consider what time will work best for each Gen Yer. Then communicate with each Gen Yer the expectation that you will meet regularly one-on-one at a regular time.

Whenever possible, try to choose a regular time and stick with it as long as you can. If you have to make a change, try to set a new regular time and try to stick with the new time as long as you can. Regularity makes a big difference to Gen Yers. In-person meetings are always preferable to meetings by telephone, but if your only option is telephone, don't let the phone call slip. Keep those telephone appointments the way you make sure to attend your own child's birthday party. And make sure to support these telephone conversations with clear point-by-point e-mails before and after your calls. Follow-up e-mails are key, especially following telephone one-on-ones.

Whenever you *can* meet in person, try to conduct your meetings in the same place. Choose a good venue, whether it is your office, a conference room, or the stairwell. You want these meetings to become familiar and comfortable. The routine of meeting in the same place every time is an important part of the structure these one-on-one meetings provide.

Making a plan with a Gen Yer to meet one-on-one at a regular time and place is a huge commitment for both of you. It is a powerful statement that you care enough to spend time setting this person up for success. When you follow through and spend that time, you are creating a constant feedback loop for ongoing short-term goal setting, performance evaluation, coaching, troubleshooting, and regular course correction.

It's also a lot of pressure on both of you. But it's good pressure.

For the employee, the pressure is that of constant account-ability. Quite literally, the employee will be expected to give an account of her performance in every one-on-one meeting. Has she met her short-term goals? Has she accomplished everything on her to-do list? Has she met all the guidelines and specifications? Has her performance been timely and swift? Have her results been high quality? Has her demeanor been cheerful and energetic? She will hope to score points—actually or metaphorically—in every meeting. Meanwhile, she will also expect feedback from you, including regular fine-tuning, revising, adjusting, and suggestions for improvement.

For you as the manager, the pressure is to carry the ball without dropping it. After all, you are the boss here. You are the one who has to make sure these one-on-ones happen, as scheduled, in the right place, and at the right time. If it is a new habit for you, this practice may feel uncomfortable or burdensome at first. It will take time to get used to it. It will be easy, on a very busy day, to look at your schedule and be tempted to skip it. Don't.

If you skip meetings, you are sending a message to Gen Yers that the schedule is not real, the structure is not solid, and the relation-ship is not reliable. They will take it as license to start skipping meetings when they feel like it. It will be very hard to reestablish the routine. So you'll feel the greatest pressure on those times when you inevitably do drop the ball. At those times, you only have one good option: "Mea culpa!" Confess and ask forgiveness. Say, "I let you down. I'm sorry. I hope you'll forgive me." Explain that it is pre-cisely the very chaos and uncertainty at work that makes the struc-ture of regularly scheduled meetings so important. Then ask, "Will you please trust me to resume our regularly scheduled meetings with discipline?" The only thing to do is to get back on schedule imme-diately, get back to work, and do better.

Create a Focused Routine for Your One-on-Ones

One Gen Yer told me, "The coolest job I ever had was working for this guy who was really intense, but he made me have these 'focus meetings' with him every day. He'd show up or call and say, 'Okay. Focus meeting. Are you ready?' It was his chance to tell me what was going on and what he needed me to put at the top of my list. It sounds terrible, but it was great. I knew it was coming every day: 'This is what's important right now.' I always knew what I was doing was important work, at least to him." I've heard this kind of testimony over and over again from Gen Yers and managers alike. Gen Yers thrive on the familiar and comfortable structure of a focused routine, especially in relationships with authority figures. The routine doesn't have to be pretty, as long as it's a routine—the faster and tidier, the better.

It won't be enough to start meeting regularly with your Gen Yers one-on-one. You'll have to teach them *how* to meet with you. Spell out how long you expect each meeting to last (my advice is to keep them to fifteen or twenty minutes). Don't ever let these meetings become long or convoluted. Make it clear that your meetings will follow a fast and tidy agenda, preferably the same basic format every time. Start each meeting by reviewing the agenda. Whenever possible, present an agenda in writing that you can both follow. These meetings should be cordial but all business. This is not the time for chitchat.

Often managers have a difficult time talking to their young employees. "I always feel like I should touch base personally before moving onto my list. It's slightly disingenuous, I guess," said one manager in a small professional office. "I might say, 'What did you do last night?' Or 'Did you see that show last night?' Or 'Did you get

> Gen Yers thrive on the familiar and comfortable structure of a focused routine, especially in relationships with authority figures.

in okay this morning? How was traffic?' But really, I'm just trying to warm up to, 'Great, here's my list.'" Don't waste these meetings shooting the breeze, pretending to be friends, or worst of all, talking about deep personal matters. These meetings should not become therapy sessions. This is not your chance to play older sibling, confidante, wise sage, or pal. Also beware of letting your regular one-on-ones digress into big-picture career discussions or long-range planning sessions. There may be a time and a place for everything, but your regular one-on-ones are not the time and place for anything but helping each Gen Yer focus on priorities in the short term. All references to matters really deep, big picture, or long term should be immediately diverted back to short-term details that can be written down on a to-do list.

Customize One-on-Ones for Every Employee

Like everything else, this dynamic process will change over time, and your approach will have to change with each young employee you meet with regularly. For each of your employees, you'll have to figure out how often to meet, how much time to spend at each meeting, what format to use, and what topics to cover. And remember: You'll have to make adjustments over time. If things are not going well with a particular Gen Yer, maybe you'll have to meet longer and more often, going over his to-do list twice a day with a fine-tooth comb. And if things are going really well with a Gen Yer, maybe you only need to meet twice a week—just long enough to check progress and troubleshoot any issues that come up with her current tasks, responsibilities, and projects. No matter how well things seem to be going, you still need to verify that things are indeed going as well as you think. If they are, make sure that Gen Yer knows just how many points she is scoring today.

Never forget that your one-on-ones are your primary method for keeping the lines of communication open. Keep your expectations on the table, and make sure you are showing them exactly how to meet and exceed your expectations. And keep asking, "What do you need from me?"

Give Them "Real" Power

"I think these Generation Y guys are power hungry," whispered a manager from the world of high finance. "They always want to know about the pecking order when it comes to who is really in charge. They want to know who controls the resources and who can really help them advance. One of the new guys asked me, 'Who do I need to listen to, and who can I ignore?' I can't help saying I thought that was pretty savvy, and I did end up telling him, 'Listen to me,' and I gave him a few other people and told him we were the only ones he really needed to keep happy. That guy is turning out really to be very sharp, and he's going to be very successful if he stays with us."

I hear stories like this all the time and not just from people in high finance or other similarly competitive industries. Recently a director in a large nonprofit organization said to me, "Every one of the Gen Yers seems to have overly inflated views of how much responsibility they should have. They think they should be able to make decisions that are really appropriate only for much more senior people with much more experience." She went on, "It's like they've always been taught to question authority, so they come in here questioning the existing hierarchy and the way decisions are made." I explained to this director that when kids grow up with parents who actually teach them how to question authority, they usually learn to be pretty good at it.

Think about this: What if your voice had been given great weight since you were a small child? Might you expect to be taken seriously? What if you grew up being able to answer just about any question instantly with the touch of a keyboard? Wouldn't you be a bit of a know-it-all? What if you watched institutions and titans and celebrities rise and fall every day? Would you really expect authority figures to be set in stone?

Gen Yers are acutely aware of power relations. One of them recently told me, "I just want to know where I stand. Who am I supposed to be taking orders from? Whose ass am I supposed to be kissing? Who is supposed to be kissing my ass? You know what I mean? What's my territory? What's my zone of power? So I can operate freely and work my magic." And they definitely want as much power as they can get their hands on. That's not just true in the workplace. That's true about any situation where they spend considerable time and care one wit about the people or the undertaking. If they spend time there and they care, they want to know: Who is in charge? Who controls the resources? And where do I stand in the pecking order?

Give Them Real Power

A very common mistake managers make is trying to humor Gen Yers. These managers want Gen Yers to spend their time and energy on concrete tasks and responsibilities. But all the while, these managers distract Gen Yers from their actual lack of power by giving them "fake" power, telling them, "You are my right-hand man" or "Do it however you think it should be done." But power in the workplace is not a pretend game to Gen Yers. As one aptly put it, "Don't tell me I'm your right-hand man and then keep me running around all day doing your personal errands. If my job is to pick up your kids after school every day and bring them to your house, I'm not exactly your right-hand man. If I'm your personal errand boy, just tell me I'm your personal errand boy. Tell me what a great job I have to do with your personal errands to get some more real work. What do I have to do to prove myself so I can get some more responsibility for real work?"

For Gen Yers, power is about control of resources, wielding of status, authority to make decisions, and autonomy to take action. In reality, they do not have the power to ignore the tasks they don't like or take on responsibilities that don't belong to them. They are not free to do things their own way or get others to do things their way. They do not have a title recognized by their coworkers as prestigious. They cannot access and deploy money or anything that costs money. Stop pretending.

> Gen Yers want power, all right. But they are not interested in fake power. They want real power.

Gen Yers want power, all right. But they are not interested in fake power. They want real power. Focus their power hunger on their real work.

If you want to give Gen Yers the power to make decisions on their own, you need to prepare them to do so. If you want to give Gen Yers the power to take action on their own, you need to spell out all the guidelines and parameters up front. You need to tell them, "If you are in situation A, follow steps 1, 2, and 3. If you are in situation B, follow steps 4, 5, and 6. If you are in situation C, follow steps 7, 8, and 9." If you want them to use their own judgment, then you have to make it clear exactly where their discretion begins and where it ends. Spell out what they can do and what they cannot and may not do.

The key to giving Gen Yers real power is to define real goals with clear guidelines and set strict deadlines with detailed time lines and regular benchmarks along the way. In between those regular benchmarks, let Gen Yers work on their own terms and in their own time. The more concrete the expectations you set up front, the greater their feeling of ownership will be. In general, the more structure you provide, the more freely Gen Yers can operate within those certain boundaries.

Lend Them Your Power to Get Things Done

There will always be unexpected obstacles, problems, and people who get in the way no matter how certain the boundaries you establish. One aerospace manager in a large manufacturing facility said to me, "I'll tell you what always messes up my guys and makes them feel powerless: When they cannot get something they need out of someone in another work group, department, or another division or sometimes an outside vendor. I'll come in and ask how things are going, and they're totally dead-ended because they are waiting to get some missing link and they are being ignored because they are peons." The manager continued, "I just tell them, 'You are peons. Nobody is afraid of you. I am just a notch above peon, but my boss, Mr. Green, is a big wheel, and I use his name to get what we need. If someone is stonewalling you, you have to let me know immediately and let me make the call so it doesn't hold up the project.' The funny thing is that I think this actually makes them a little cocky, like, 'Do we need to get Mr. Green involved in this?' But it actually makes them more powerful and things get done."

I can't recommend telling your young employees they are peons, but I highly recommend telling it like it is. These are lessons I've learned from many wise leaders of Gen Yers in the real world:

- Teach them how to get things done in your organization.
- Let them know where they truly stand in relation to others.
- Make it clear that you are a power source in their working life, and lend them some of your power to help them get things done.

One senior partner in a consulting firm helped me put a fine point on these lessons by sharing this example: "Our problem is that you can have a perfectly solid working relationship with an associate, then another partner will swoop down and dump work on him. All of a sudden, I'm not getting the work out of this associate, even though I see he's here until all hours of the night. I'll say, 'Did you tell Mr. Jones you were working on this matter for me?' He'll just look overwhelmed and tell me, 'I told him that, and he said this was very important and he really needed me to do it.' So what am I supposed to say?" This senior partner continued, "What I came to realize was that the younger associates think they can't say no—and in fact they don't want to. The more partners they work for, the more decision makers they are winning over, the more power they are connected to. But that means they are always caught in the middle trying to set priorities when they really have no way to know what should take priority. Now I tell associates whenever I give them an assignment, 'If another partner tries to give you an assignment, here's what I want you to do. First thing you do is tell him you are working on this matter for me with a tight deadline. Second thing you do is tell him I told you that you do not have the authority to put his assignment ahead of mine. Tell him to call me to discuss the competing assignments. Third thing you do is text-message me immediately to tell me. I'm your panic button.' It's just not fair for us to expect these brand-new associates to set priorities on assignments. We have to help them do that."

Lessons learned: Prepare Gen Yers for the expected. Then counsel them to expect the unexpected. Give them a standard course of action in the face of the unexpected. In case of emergency, you may have to be their panic button.

Create an Upward Spiral of Continuous Improvement

Managers often tell me they have a hard time talking to Gen Yers about failures great and small. "When they make a mistake, you hesitate to tell them because they take it so hard," I was told by a partner at a prestigious law firm. "They seem to take it personally, like you are breaking their heart. I want to say, 'Don't feel bad. Just go back and make these changes, and then next time try to remember to do it properly in the first place.' That seems pretty basic." It is pretty basic.

When it comes to addressing Gen Yers' performance problems, the most common mistake managers make is soft-pedaling honest feedback or withholding it altogether. Sometimes managers take back incomplete work and finish it themselves or reassign it. Other times the problems are not addressed at all, and the work product remains substandard. Gen Yers are left to fail unwittingly or improve on their own impulse and initiative. As one Gen Yer put it, "What do you want me to do, scream it? Beg for it? Help! Help me get it right. Help me do it faster. Help me do it better. Help me improve."

The second most common mistake managers make when dealing with Gen Yers' performance problems is hit-and-run criticism. Unlike soft-pedaling managers, hit-and-run managers don't hesitate to offer honest negative comments about Gen Yers' performance. But hit-and-run managers often critique work randomly—when they happen to notice a mistake and also have a moment to reach out to the employee in question—instead of systematically reviewing work product. They are likely to disparage errors and omissions, even when they haven't taken the time earlier to make expectations clear. Gen Yers usually feel blindsided. One Gen Yer shared this story with me: "There was this one guy who would just attack me out of the blue. I wasn't even working for him, really, but he was on the project. I'd see him in the cafeteria, and he would grab my upper arm and tell me something I did was crap: 'Your presentation this morning was crap.' 'That e-mail you sent around this morning was crap.' I hated that guy."

When it comes to performance management with Gen Yers, the best practice is to be systematic, honest, and positive. That's how you create an upward spiral of continuous improvement.

Focus on Solutions, Not Problems

"I learned early on that the trick with Generation Y is exactly NOT to ignore performance problems, exactly NOT to tell them they are doing better than they are. But you can't ambush them either. It has to be a process of continuous improvement." That's what I was told by one of the most successful business leaders in the restaurant industry—a man with a reputation for developing young, high-potential employees into industry superstars. "When I am developing a young talent, I spend a lot of time focusing on problems, one little problem after another. I don't sugar-coat it, but I never treat it like a problem." He continued, "No matter what they do, they know my focus is next steps."

I could see why this guy was so successful at developing Gen Yers. He continued, "They want to improve, even the less talented, less promising young men and women. If you talk about continuous improvement, they are all ears. You can't ignore problems because that's really what continuous improvement is: Removing imperfections one at a time. But I never bother calling it a problem. For me, it's all about next steps. I have a district manager I'm trying to move up quickly to regional manager. His general managers have been way over on their labor budgets, which tells me he is not focusing on their labor budgets. So we went over the numbers, but I never said a word about it being a problem. I just told him, 'Let's talk about next steps. For the next two weeks, I want you to call every general manager in your district every day to remind them to focus on controlling the labor budget in their restaurant. Set aside your whole morning for that if you have to, but I want you to call every one of them every day for the next two weeks.'"

This manager explained, "I'm not focusing on the problem. I'm focusing him on the solution. That's what continuous improvement really is anyway. It's always about whatever we are focused on improving at the moment. I find that when they have a whole bunch of next steps focused on solutions, that problem not only gets solved, but it doesn't come back, not with that person anyway. It's not just a great way to improve at the moment. It's a great way for them to fill in that gap in their performance. They learn the lesson, and it sticks."

This "next steps" focus is one level deeper than a "results focus." Next steps will help you concentrate your performance management efforts on the concrete actions within the control of each individual employee. Maintaining a next-steps focus requires a constant accounting. Keep asking your young employees: Exactly what concrete actions—next steps—are you going to take next? What can you do to improve? What do you need to revise and adjust?

Keep Track of Their Performance

The challenge with this deep level of performance management is how to monitor performance closely enough to make fair and accurate evaluations and to provide the guidance necessary to facilitate constant improvement. There is no substitute for actually watching Gen Yers performing their concrete actions.

"It's kind of like going to my kid's Little League game," said one retail manager. "I learn more about my employees from watching them deal with a customer for a few minutes than almost any other performance indicator." I call this approach *shadowing*. Any time an employee is struggling with a recurring performance problem, shadow that employee for a little while and watch him in action. Nine times out of ten, you'll be able to help the employee solve the problem with relative ease by focusing on next steps. But it is the rare manager who can regularly watch employees work with his or her own eyes.

You must have a way to monitor and measure their performance on a regular basis. That means you need to spot-check their work. Ask customers for feedback on individual employees. Ask other managers. And ask Gen Yers themselves. As one Gen Yer said: "I'd rather have a manager who is keeping really close track of what I'm doing than one who doesn't know who I am or what I'm doing or even care. My boss trusts me to keep really close track of myself, which is what I want. I'm the one doing all the talking. I tell her everything I'm doing in a weekly report. I have a running list so it's easy. I e-mail her which things are done and what I'm working on at the present time. Then we go over it on the phone. She trusts me, and I am a total star for her."

One of the best approaches I've seen to the challenge of monitoring Gen Yers' performance is making them responsible for keeping track of their own performance. Give Gen Yers tools like project plans, work diaries, and checklists. Ask them to keep track of their own work in writing and report to you on a regular basis. "I have them write down everything," said the manager of an entry-level group in a large insurance company. "I have them keep track of their whole day in an activity log. Most of them find it very helpful. For me, I couldn't function without it because I have twenty-six people. I

> You must have a way to monitor and measure Gen Yers' performance on a regular basis.

can help them track down just about any problem any time because I say, 'Let's just go through your activity log and see what happened.' My group is the least experienced one in this entire company, and our error rate is the lowest. I attribute that entirely to the activity logs. What they love is being the highest-performing group and the rewards that come with that." I asked, "Exactly what was it about those activity logs that made such a difference?" "We use the logs to go back and find errors, eliminate the errors, and prevent the errors from recurring. But the biggest impact is how it impacts their work. It slows them down and forces them to double- and triple-check their work. Just keeping the activity logs makes them more careful."

The best managers I know create a constant feedback loop with their Gen Yers—what one very experienced manager in information technology calls "coming full circle." He said, "That's my mantra with them: 'Come full circle with that.' What that means is, 'This assignment begins with a conversation between you and me, and it's going to come back to a conversation between you and me. I'm going to want to know what happened. Did you do what I asked you to do? Did you do it the way I asked you to do it? If not, why not? Did anything come up that I hadn't anticipated? Did you think of a better way? So come full circle, and we'll talk about what happened.' That's what it means to me."

When I interviewed this manager's Gen Y employees, they all said the same thing, "Oh yeah, 'Come full circle!' That's his mantra." I wasn't surprised that they all seemed to appreciate coming full circle. One of the young programmers told me, "Basically that's how he helps us help ourselves. You'd think it was him being a control freak, always asking us tons of questions and keeping such close tabs on everything we are doing. But I'm starting to think he doesn't even keep as close tab as he seems to. I think it's really about keeping us on our toes." Another programmer on this manager's team told me, "He definitely knows exactly what everyone is doing all the time. But it's his secret weapon. He doesn't want anyone leaving loose ends hanging out there. So you always are second-guessing yourself, making sure you haven't forgotten anything, or left any loose ends because he is definitely going to ask you about it." Yet another programmer on the team told me, "He calls it coming full circle, but it never ends. He's always there with you. It's more like an upward spiral."

Teach Them How to Get What They Need from You

Managers often tell me that Gen Yers make a lot of requests and demands. I say those Gen Yers are doing you a favor. Once you know what they want from you, you have the key to getting what you want from them. Case in point: One Gen Yer told me, "I cannot work Friday, Saturday, or Sunday. I know that sucks, but I can't. The thing is, I'll do anything else. Give me Fridays, Saturdays, and Sundays, and I'll do anything else, and I mean anything. I'll wade through a river of shit." Stop taking insult when Gen Yers make demands and requests. Start using that opportunity to drive their performance.

"I tell my Gen Yers, 'If you want to carry some weight with me, you've got to bring your very best effort to work every day,'" an experienced mechanical service contractor told me. "'You've got to get here early and stay late. Don't screw around while you are on a job. When you are here in the shop, find something to make yourself useful. If you see something out of place, fix it. If you see one of the other guys screwing around, tell him to knock it off. Take some initiative. Keep moving. I'm right here. I know who's been naughty and who's been nice. You want to carry weight with me, carry your weight around here.'" When I talked to some of the Gen Yers who worked for this contractor, they all nodded in agreement, and one of them said, "There is no doubt. The slack-offs wouldn't dare ask him for anything. But the really hard workers have no doubt that he'll do anything for us."

That's the key: Spell out for your Gen Yers exactly what they must do to get your assistance in getting their needs met. Help them help you help them.

One health care executive offered this approach: "You want something from me? Before you ask me for something, I want to know: What is the benefit of what you are proposing? Is there a benefit to me? To the company? To the group? Who benefits? What does it take to make this happen? What role are you going to play in all of this? Who else is going to be involved? How long is this going to take? Where is this going to happen? How are you going to do it? Just answer those questions for me."

> Spell out for your Gen Yers exactly what they must do to get your assistance in getting their needs met. Help them help you help them.

Indeed, by requiring that an employee who makes a request answer these questions, you are in effect helping that person prepare a simple proposal. I have seen this technique work wonders for managers of Gen Y in organizations of all shapes and sizes. When managers require Gen Yers to put requests in the form of a simple proposal, Gen Yers tend to make fewer requests, make more reasonable requests, and make their requests in a much more professional manner. No matter how simple the process is, the very act of stopping to put their requests into a proposal format causes Gen Yers to consider those requests more carefully. "Don't make requests lightly, and they won't be taken lightly," is how an enlisted leader in the U.S. Marine Corps put it. This genuine war hero told me, "If my Marines ask me for something, I'm going to break my back to get it for them. So don't make requests lightly, please. Requests are serious business."

A great sage in the financial services industry told me, "Young analysts are always in my office asking me for this or that. I have a simple rule now: Give me a proposal. You want a paper clip? Give me a proposal. That one could be a very short proposal. But that's my response to everything, and it has trickled right back down. Ask your team leader for a paper clip in my division, and your team leader is going to say, 'Give me a proposal!'" I asked her if she was creating needless red tape—her own little internal bureaucracy. "No, no, no," she insisted. "There's no red tape. There's no bureaucracy. We want them to stop and think before they ask for this or that. It could be a sentence, a paragraph, a page. Just make a persuasive case."

She added, "It's great training for them, anyway. You have to be able to make a persuasive business case to make things happen. When it comes to getting resources out of administration, or getting resources out of people in other divisions, my analysts are light-years ahead because they know how to make a persuasive business case. They actually bring resources into our division most of the time rather than soaking up my resources. They go forth into the firm and gather up resources, one proposal after another."

I've seen the proposal technique used by managers formally, informally, and inadvertently. It works like a charm. I've seen managers use it to help Gen Yers get more resources for their own work or the work of their team; greater financial rewards for themselves or their subordinates; greater access to perks; credit for results achieved; new tasks, responsibilities, or projects; special assignments; training opportunities; exposure to decision makers; the chance to work in a choice location; scheduling flexibility; and the quirkiest personal accommodations you can imagine.

Even while managers are helping Gen Yers get more of what they need and want, the proposal technique also helps managers ensure that Gen Yers are paying a fair market value—in time and hard work—for whatever it is they are getting. "Maybe they are getting more than their fair share," says the wise sage, "Good for them! This is business. We are trying to turn a profit. So are they!"

For years in my seminars, I've been teaching managers to use one version or another of the proposal technique with Gen Yers, especially when it comes to using rewards—great and small—to drive performance. It's not enough to define expectations clearly and tie concrete rewards directly to the fulfillment of those expectations. The more open and transparent the process for earning rewards of any kind, the more the rewards will drive performance. That's why the proposal technique works so well. In effect, it turns Gen Yers' requests and demands upside down so they become opportunities for Gen Yers to earn performance-based rewards.

•   •

Oh, yes, I should point out another important reason to teach Gen Yers to manage themselves and help them earn more of what they want/need from you. If they get what they want/need from you, they are less likely to leave.

CHAPTER NINE

RETAIN THE BEST OF GEN Y, ONE DAY AT A TIME

> I guess I would stay as long as they keep making it work for me. I'm not committed to leaving this place on any timetable. Let's take it one day at a time. Who knows? Maybe I'll end up working my whole life in this place after all.
>
> —Gen Yer

W e have an elaborate recruiting apparatus that gives us a huge presence on college and university campuses," said one senior executive in a major financial services firm. "We are known for our fast-track program, so we get a huge number of applicants and we put them through this meticulous screening process. After we hire them, we invest a huge amount in them right away over the course of the first year because we truly believe they are the future of the company. Still, by the end of the second year, half of them are gone. Most of them leave to go work for another financial services firm, and the competition is happy to have them precisely because they've been through our fast-track program. It's so frustrating. It seems that that no matter what we do, we just can't keep them."

I hear different versions of this story from leaders and managers in every industry. Leaders and managers are very worried about high levels of turnover among Gen Yers, and they are right to be. In most organizations, turnover among new employees has been going up ever so slightly but steadily over the past two decades. Turnover is by far the highest among employees with zero to two years' tenure and next highest among employees with two to five years' tenure. Is this partly a function of youth and the unsettled nature of early career positions? Yes. Is it also a reflection of overall labor trends toward shorter periods of employment? Yes.

But there are also generational issues at play here. Gen Yers are coming of age in a labor market that presumes total job mobility. Meanwhile, Gen Yers are more likely than those of earlier generations to see the job as just one piece in their life puzzle rather than as the first, indispensable anchor piece without which they cannot build a happy life and family. To Gen Yers seeking to customize the perfect life and career, the job is a less important puzzle piece than, say, where they live, what schedule they keep, opportunities to participate in certain activities, proximity to friends or family. Add all these factors together, and it's easy to see that Gen Yers are likely to have the highest early career stage turnover of any generation in history.

But is it impossible to retain the best of Generation Y? No. You can retain the best people indefinitely, "one day at a time," as long as you are willing to keep making it work for them. You can even turn many of the best into long-term employees and some of the very best into new leaders. You have no choice. They *are* the future of your organization.

Instead of Trying to Eliminate Turnover, Take Control of It

When my phone rings, there is often a desperate business leader on the other end of the phone. She will sometimes start rattling off numbers, but usually the message is simple: "Turnover among our new employees is up. We want to bring it down. Help!" The reason these leaders are desperate is that high turnover among this group is extremely costly.

- When you lose an employee, you incur the additional cost of recruiting a replacement.

- You lose (often to your competitor) the formal or informal training dollars you have invested in that person.

- When you lose a relatively new employee, the loss of the training investment is exacerbated because employers spend the bulk of their training investment in the first stages of a new employee's employment. What is more, the sooner a new employee leaves after receiving that training investment, the less time the organization has had to reap a return on that investment.

- When any employee leaves voluntarily, there is a disruption in work flow and work relationships on the team. Some employees leave suddenly and not well, and as a result, the disruption is greater.

- A new employee's leaving sometimes triggers other new employees to leave too.

- The greater your turnover among the newly hired, the less robust is your supply chain of potential home-grown new leaders up the ranks.

Yes, high turnover is bad. But not *all* turnover is bad. That's why my response to desperate business leaders facing high turnover is usually to ask three questions: "Who is staying?" "Who is going?" and "Who is deciding?"

Your goal should not be to eliminate turnover among Gen Yers. That's never going to happen. Your goal should be to take control of the turnover among Gen Yers. You want the high performers to stay and the low performers to go. The only way to make that happen is if you are the one deciding who stays and who goes. How do you achieve that?

> Your goal should be to take control of the turnover among Gen Yers. You want the high performers to stay and the low performers to go.

One key to gaining control is the prestige factor. Gen Yers are highly aware of prestige and status, and they want to be associated with them. A Gen Yer recently told me, "I want to be part of a prestige group. I don't want to be associated with some second-rate anything. Are you the best? Is this a place where just anyone can work? Where is your prestige factor?" In order to retain the best, you need to send the message that "not everyone gets to work here" and that "it is a privilege and an honor to work here."

Very few organizations achieve outstanding prestige as employers: McKinsey & Company, the GE Audit Program, the U.S. Marine Corps, Google, and Enterprise Rent-a-Car, to name a handful of employers in this select group. I could name plenty of others in various industries with vastly different missions and a wide range of corporate cultures. What these organizations have in common is that they are superpower employment brands among Generation Y. Why? They all have reputations for being extremely demanding, highly competitive, and fiercely merit based. They all have reputations for shining a bright light of scrutiny on the organization and on every single person working there.

Maybe you don't work for a blockbuster employment brand. Even if you don't, here is the good news: you can be the manager who sends the message, "It is a privilege and an honor to work here!" Shine that bright light of scrutiny on yourself as a leader and on every single person you manage. Hold everyone to a higher standard, and help everyone meet that higher standard. Set up a constant loop of challenge and evaluation.

What else can you do to increase the status and prestige of working for you on your team?

Push Out the Low Performers

What you can do is shine that bright light on the very top performers. But you should also shine a bright light on everyone else. In fact, you should be prepared to spend the bulk of your time working with the vast majority of employees who fall somewhere in the middle of the performance spectrum. Meanwhile, with a bright light shining on them, the stubborn low performers will usually stick out like sore thumbs. Remember: Part of sending the message that "it's a privilege and an honor to work here" is sending the message that "not everyone gets to work here!" If you are serious about retaining Gen Yers, one of the most important questions you should be asking yourself is how you can get turnover to skyrocket among the low performers.

For many years, Juan has run a small house-painting business, employing about a dozen painters. He told me this story about a young crew of four painters he was managing a few years ago: "They were all in their early twenties, except the older one was almost thirty. He had been with me for less than a year, but I made him the foreman. That's when the trouble started." Juan explained that the three younger members of the crew complained regularly about the foreman. According to them, the foreman insisted that they work from 8:00 A.M. to 4:00 P.M., because those were the hours he preferred. The younger members of the crew preferred starting at 9:00 or 10:00 A.M. and working later, which coincided with customers' preferences as well. But the young painters' most serious complaint was that the foreman was not doing any work: The foreman met them at 8:00 A.M., split the tasks for the day into three, and spent most of the day talking on his cell phone. Juan said, "If just one of them had been talking behind his back, I might not have paid attention. But they were all telling me the same thing. I thought I better start showing up at the jobs to see what was up."

Sure enough, whenever Juan dropped in on the job, he found the foreman walking around the customer's yard talking on his cell phone while the other painters were up on ladders working. Said Juan, "I decided I better start showing up at the beginning of the day and making sure that all four of them had work to do. Instead of having the foreman divide up the work three ways, I divided up the work four ways in the morning. Then I'd come by sometime during the day to see what was up. It didn't take long for me to see what the other guys were saying. Then I started really pressing the foreman, whenever I talked with him, to tell me how much of the work he was actually doing. He was gone within two weeks."

Remember that stubborn low performers hate the bright light of scrutiny and usually will find a way to escape. You rarely have to fire them if you are willing to shine that bright light. I cannot tell you how many leaders and managers have told me stories about stubborn low performers who "fire themselves" after just days or weeks of the sustained bright light.

What did Juan do with the rest of the crew? "I asked the guys what they wanted to do. They had already discussed it. They wanted to work 10:00 A.M. to 7:00 P.M. on the jobs instead of 8:00 to 4:00, and they asked if the three of them could split the foreman's pay since they were going to be doing the work of a four-man crew. I told them I'd split it with them, and I did. They each made an extra hundred bucks plus a week. They couldn't have been more pleased to have that guy gone. One of those young guys is still with me, running crews, and he's really valuable to me. He runs the crews, and I've been able to work much less."

Once you push out the stubborn low performers, the trick is getting everyone else to want to stay and work even harder for you. How? Keep shining that bright light. While low performers squirm under bright light, high performers usually shine brightest under the bright light. They want to know that someone knows just how much great work they are doing. One Gen Yer told me, "My boss finally fired this kid. He looked at all of us like we were going to freak out on him. We were all bumping fists, high-fiving, and like, 'Yo, man! What took you so long to fire this kid?' It was like, 'Okay, man, now you got my attention. Now maybe I can respect you.'"

Don't Let Good People Get into Downward Spirals

What about that vast group of employees who fall somewhere in the middle of the performance spectrum? Your job is to use that bright light of scrutiny to help them see their targets at work more clearly and aim better at those targets. By shining a bright light on their work, you tell them they are important and their work is important. Best of all, you will help them work a little faster and a little better.

We see this in our research all the time. So often Gen Yers, particularly those in the middle of the performance spectrum, lose interest in a job or start having negative feelings about an organization because they are struggling with the work. One Gen Yer shared her experience: "If I feel like I'm having a hard time doing the job, if I do not understand something, or if I keep getting stuck, that is a big demoralizer. That makes me feel much less into the job. Maybe this isn't a good place for me to succeed. I don't want to do a job where I feel like I'm failing." These young employees feel frustrated at their inability to adequately learn a skill, perform a task, or get comfortable with a responsibility. Maybe they become weighed down by a particularly challenging project. That's usually the beginning of a downward spiral for these midlevel performers. Often they decide to leave long before they tell you. As a result, the downward spiral spins out of control. By the time they leave, you might think, "Good riddance!"

How do you stop the downward spiral? Start an upward spiral instead.

In these cases, the number one thing a manager can do is help the employee improve so he will start feeling better about the job and regain interest. Use the bright light of scrutiny to help the employee see what's going wrong and how to make things go better. Break down the project, responsibility, task, or skill into small pieces. Guide and direct the employee in accomplishing one very small piece at a time. Instead of suffering the pain of failure, the employee will get a chance to bank one tiny success after another. In the process, the employee is likely to learn and grow, and feel increasingly competent. You'll also put that employee in a much stronger position to earn more of the rewards he needs. Even more

> Gen Yers start thinking about leaving a job as soon as they start thinking they might not be able to get their needs and wants met.

important, you'll restore the employee's hope about his future potential for advancement and success in this job and your company—and greater earning potential. Gen Yers feel much better about a job when they feel they are winning as opposed to losing. The problem is that you can't make them feel that they are winning just by telling them they are. You actually have to do the hard work of helping them start winning. That's how you shift the momentum and start creating an upward spiral.

Turn the Reasons Gen Yers Might Leave into Reasons They Will Stay—and Work Even Harder

Gen Yers start thinking about leaving a job as soon as they start thinking they might not be able to get their needs and wants met. If they suspect their boss doesn't know or care what they want and need, Gen Yers get nervous. The moment they conclude that their boss will not work with them to help them meet their wants and needs, Gen Yers will be halfway out the door. That's true for high performers, low performers, and everybody in the middle. At that point, you should hope they leave soon rather than stick around for months on end with one foot out the door.

Managers are sometimes offended that Gen Yers have needs and wants and expect their bosses to help them meet those needs and wants. I often tell managers that it's a transactional relationship. No hard feelings. "My boss just wouldn't do business with me. He'd look at me as if I had no right to expect anything from him," a Gen Yer recently told me. "His approach was, 'You get what I decide you get when I decide you get it.' Well, if you won't do business with me, I'm not going to do business with you." Gen Yers are coming to work to earn. Part of your job is to help them earn. And that's the key to retention. You have to turn the reasons Gen Yers leave into reasons they will stay and work harder.

Find Out What You Can Do to Keep Them

Don't wait until Gen Yers start thinking about leaving to ask, "Is there anything we can do to keep you?" Ask on the first day of employment and keep asking every single day. Does that mean you should do everything for everybody? No. Should you cater to their every whim? No. But Gen Yers need to know that somebody knows what they want and need, somebody cares, and somebody is going to work with them to help them earn more of it. The key is not to give them false hope or make false promises. When Gen Yers express needs and wants that are totally unrealistic, you should let them know that immediately so that their expectations are clear. The next step, however, is to help them see what is realistic.

"Half the time, what they want is impossible and it's a non-starter," said a manager in an agricultural sciences company. "But the other half—what they want—is easy. You want to leave early this afternoon to visit your grandmother in the hospital? What manager would say no to that? I've got managers who say no to small one-time accommodations and then, guess what? The next day that person is gone." Small one-time accommodations are easy to grant and usually a matter of kindness. Failure to grant them usually costs much more than granting them. But of course, you can't let employees take advantage.

This manager continued: "If you want to leave early every afternoon to visit your grandmother in the hospital, then that's not a one-time accommodation. That's a special schedule. Don't get me wrong. I've got chemistry technicians who are really good at their jobs, and they are hard to replace. As far as I'm concerned, they can work in the middle of the night if they want to. I'll do just about anything I can do to keep them happy because they are so valuable to me. I tell them off the bat when they come to work here, 'Tell me what you need. I'm here to facilitate your work. If you are not happy, you need to come tell me. If you need something, you need to come tell me.' Of course, some of them do and some of them don't. It's the ones who don't come tell me that I really have to worry about. I have to go ask them once in a while."

Do Whatever It Takes to Hold On to the Best and the Brightest

The reality is that you can't do everything for everybody. Otherwise where does it end? The agricultural sciences manager told me, "I've lost some really good technicians lately just because they were exhausted, burned out. They didn't want to be working so hard. They're young. They want to have some fun. After that happened a few times, I realized that I had to find a way to give these guys a break. They didn't have any vacation to speak of, and our work load wasn't getting any lighter. In one case I was going to HR to try to get one guy on a part-time status for a few months at his request. Finally, I told him to just quit and reapply whenever he was ready. It was a risk for both of us. But after about four months, he was in my office. Talk about loyalty. This guy would walk the plank for me."

Is this manager going too far? I don't think so. Once the organization has invested in recruiting and training an employee, management has a huge stake in retaining that person—even if not as a full-time, on-site, uninterrupted, exclusive employee. If you can't keep the whole employee, why not keep as much as you can? Instead of losing them, offer valued employees the chance to take an unpaid sabbatical, to work part-time or flextime or as telecommuters or consultants. When valued people leave, stay in touch with them and on good terms. Try re-recruiting them after they've had a chance to rest or after they've had a chance to see that the grass isn't so much greener on the other side.

"I have to do whatever it takes to retain key technical talent. I get slammed if one of my good chemistry technicians leaves the company," the same manager explained. "Actually we have all kinds of incentives in place to make sure we don't hoard good talent on our teams, to make sure we export good people around to different opportunities within the company. We are given pretty strong incentives to give our best people opportunities to take on new challenges within the company—whether that means moving to a new geographical area or to a different kind of role or a whole different business within the company." As a result, the manager explained, "people can reinvent themselves and their careers" without leaving the organization. If one of your best people really wants a new challenge, a new set of tasks, new learning opportunities, new work relationships, or even just a change of scenery, maybe you can help that person find what she is looking for without ever leaving the company. As hard as it might be for you as a manager to lose a talented employee on your team, that is a giant service to the company and the individual. They definitely remember that you helped them at a key point in their career."

The lesson: Start talking with Gen Yers about retention on day one, and keep talking about it. If you are talking with them about how to meet their needs and wants on an ongoing basis, they are much more likely to talk with you at those key points when they are trying to decide whether to leave or stay. If you are willing to work with them, you can be flexible and generous. That's how you make them want to stay and work harder, at least for a little while longer. Years from now, the Gen Yers who turn out to be long-term employees will be the ones who decided over and over again that they wanted to stay a little while longer.

Go the Extra Mile to Keep the Top Performers

"The worst thing is when we lose the very good ones," said a senior partner in a major law firm. "Sometimes it's the very best among the young lawyers who leave us in the first two or three years. That's when we question ourselves. There are plenty of situations in which we would have been willing to do much more for certain people in order to keep them. We would have given them significant salary and bonus increases or cut a year off their partner track, move them to a different office. There are a lot of things we can do for people. There are some we would have been willing to negotiate with in order to keep them." Why don't they do that? "By the time they tell you they are leaving, they usually have accepted another offer. The ones who are worth more have no problem getting very generous offers from other firms. That's the point."

That is exactly the point. Your best Gen Yers have the most options and are not about to accept less than they think they are worth. "I know what I can get out there, of course," a Gen Yer told me. "We all do. If you care at all, you can find out what just about anyone makes. We all keep track of that stuff." Remember that most Gen Yers have a high opinion of their worth. The winners know they are worth a winner's lot. You might want to start negotiating with them before it's too late.

Yes, some employees are more valuable than others—to you as a manager, to your team, and to the organization. I promise you Gen Yers know this as well, and the real winners know it best of all. Not everyone gets a trophy, but the winners will be expecting them—lots of them. And they'll want valuable rewards to go along with those trophies. It follows that the more valuable the employee in question, the greater your retention efforts should be.

Make a point of talking regularly with your very best Gen Yers. Don't just ask them, "Are you happy here?" Rather, talk to them regularly to find out what they really want or need—whether it's a special deal or a small accommodation. Understanding an individual employee's unique needs or wants is the key to being able to reward that person in a meaningful way. The more unusual the needs and wants of a particular employee, the more valuable it will be if you are able to meet those needs and wants, because it

> Not everyone gets a trophy, but the winners will be expecting them— lots of them.

will be harder for other employers to replicate these unusual rewards. If you can work out a special deal with a star Gen Yer to meet some unusual need or want that really matters to that person, you will have a powerful retention tool. Of course, you have to keep asking because their needs and wants are likely to change over time.

Whatever you are doing to be flexible and generous to retain your good employees, you need to be much more flexible and generous to keep your great employees. Ask yourself the following questions:

- What are you paying your good employees? Pay your great ones more. Consider giving them more in base pay and benefits. Definitely give them more bonus money contingent on clear performance benchmarks tied directly to concrete actions they can control.

- What kind of scheduling flexibility are you providing for your good employees? Give your great ones the best schedules, and give them more control over when they work.

- How are your good employees assigned to work with vendors, customers, coworkers, subordinates, and managers? Give your great employees first choice in relationship opportunities at work.

- How are tasks and responsibilities assigned to good employees? Give your great employees first choice. Give the great ones first choice on any special projects or choice assignments.

- What training opportunities are being made available to good employees? Offer the best training resources to the best people first.

- How are good employees assigned to work locations or work spaces? What about travel? Give the best people the first choice of location, work space, and travel.

Every Gen Yer wants a custom deal. The more you are able to customize for them, the longer you will keep them. But if your resources and your ability to customize are limited, you had better concentrate those resources on your very best people. That's only fair. And it's the only way you are going to retain the best Gen Yers for any reasonable duration of employment.

Providing more generous rewards and work conditions in order to reward and retain high performers is a growing workplace trend. Business leaders understand it because it dovetails with the strong trends toward employee ranking and pay for performance. What we've learned in our research is that providing differential rewards works only when managers do the hard work of shining that bright light of scrutiny on every employee. Every single employee needs to understand how and why she is earning her rewards and what she needs to do in order to earn more. That means defining expectations every step of the way and tying concrete rewards directly to the fulfillment of those expectations.

When your employees deliver on their commitments for you, you deliver on promised rewards for them. If they fail to meet commitments, you have to call them on that failure immediately and withhold the reward. When every person is managed this way, your employees are much less likely to wonder why another person is receiving special rewards. They all know that someone who is receiving some special reward must have earned it fair and square.

Give the Superstars the Most Time and Attention

"I am repeatedly taken aback when I look at which consultants have stayed and which ones have left in recent years," said a senior executive in a major consulting firm. "I sit in on team meetings or client engagement sessions. I read performance evaluations. I talk to the senior managers. I take small groups to lunch. I can always tell the high potentials. I used to be able to predict with pretty good certainty which ones would stay. But in recent years, I have been repeatedly surprised. It seems like too many of the high potentials are leaving within the first few years now. That is something we need to turn around."

What can be done to turn it around? The senior executive continued: "Our culture is such that if you are really doing a great job, you are less likely to have contact with your senior manager. The senior managers probably spend too much time on a few low performers, whereas they spend very little time interfacing with the fast learner who immediately gets with the program, stays busy, and solves his own problems as they come up. If you are a senior manager and one or two of your consultants know how to pick up work and make themselves useful, you are grateful to have a couple of people you don't have to worry about. The problem is that you don't worry about those high potentials because you figure they don't really need you. And then you find out they are leaving. One day it seems that everything is going great with this person. The next day that person is leaving."

This is a common situation. Taking their cues from the workplace of the past, many leaders and managers look at their best Gen Y employees and think what they always have thought: The self-starting high performers must be the employees most likely to stay here and thrive. Surely they must know they are doing well here. They must understand that no news is good news. They must realize that as long as they keep doing more work and better work than everybody else, in the long run, they will be rewarded.

Does it work? No. Not anymore.

Don't make the mistake of thinking that some of your Gen Yers are so talented, skilled, and motivated that they don't really need the attention of managers. As one Gen Yer put it, "If you expect me to believe I am one of the best in my class, then why would you totally ignore me? You tell me I'm the future of the company, but you don't give me the time of day? How do you expect me to interpret that?" The better they are, the more attention they want: The superstar Gen Yers want managers who know exactly who they are, help them succeed, and keep close track of their success.

"We realize the high potentials need a lot more time and attention than we've typically given them. But it's not always clear who the right person is to give them that time and attention. Is it the

> Any manager who is weak, disengaged, and out of the loop will seem completely unworthy to high-potential Gen Yers.

manager or the senior manager on the project? Should we assign them mentors who stick with them over time regardless of what they are working on?" We hear this conundrum often from leaders and managers. What is the solution? We recommend focusing on four types of developmental relationships in order to surround Gen Y superstars with high concentrations of time and attention.

Teaching-Style (or Coaching-Style) Managers

Any leader, manager, or supervisor who is charged with managing any person on any project for any period of time has an obligation to play this role. But it's doubly important with Gen Yers and triply important with the best Gen Yers. Any manager who is weak, disengaged, and out of the loop will seem completely unworthy to high-potential Gen Yers. This will cause the superstar to quickly lose confidence in the organization and the chain of command. Superstar Gen Yers want managers who know and care enough to teach them the tricks and the shortcuts, warn them of pitfalls, and help them solve problems. They want managers who are strong enough to support them through bad days and counsel them through difficult judgment calls. And even more than average Gen Yers, the superstars want to know that someone is keeping track of their great work and looking for ways to provide them with special rewards.

Mentors

Many organizations try to put in place mentoring programs. The idea is to match promising Gen Yers with older, more experienced people in the organization. But mentoring means different things to different people. To many, mentoring evokes a deeply personal relationship that requires a natural connection between mentor and protégé that often takes a long time to develop. In this view, you usually wouldn't know who your real mentors are except in retrospect. Who has shared with you the rich lessons of their own lives over the course of many years? Which of those relationships have been profound and formative for you? Many argue that this type of relationship shouldn't be forced. So what can you do as an organization to promote this kind of mentoring? Encourage older, more experienced leaders to seek protégés and help these would-be mentors develop some of the techniques and habits of mentoring. Encourage younger, less experienced high-potential employees to seek mentors and help these would-be protégés develop some of the techniques and habits of being a good protégé. Perhaps you could hold matchmaking sessions including would-be mentors and would-be protégés and help them gravitate toward each other. One word of caution: The big lesson I've taken away from the dozens of corporate mentoring initiatives I've studied is that *mentoring* is usually the wrong word. I think it is usually the case, when organizations launch "mentoring" programs, that what they are really talking about is matching high-potential Gen Yers with what I would call career advisers and organizational supporters.

Career Advisers

These are more experienced (usually older) leaders and managers within the organization who will make a commitment to be available to one or more Gen Y superstars to provide career advice. The adviser meets with the Gen Yer on a regular basis to talk strategically about how the Gen Yer should navigate her career within the organization. They might discuss how the Gen Yer's work assignments have been going and what assignments should be sought next. They might discuss what the Gen Yer could do within the organization to request new training opportunities, transfers to new work groups, or moves to new locations. The career adviser might recommend strategies for pursuing raises, promotions, or desired work conditions or might counsel the Gen Yer to delay such requests until a more opportune moment. The idea is to offer the Gen Yer regular career advice from an insider's perspective so they don't have to get it from outsiders (like headhunters).

Organizational Supporters

This is like an internal career adviser with some clout. Organizational supporters don't just discuss career strategies. They actually use their influence and authority within the organization to make sure that the most valuable Gen Yers are getting the lion's share of resources to support and accelerate their career success. Typically organizational supporters talk regularly with their high-potential Gen Yers to make certain that nothing has gone wrong or is going wrong in their work assignments. They steer their Gen Y superstars to the best training opportunities, the choice projects and assignments, and the most powerful decision makers. They help fast-track their Gen Y superstars to help them win bonuses, raises, promotions, and desired work conditions. The idea is to make certain the Gen Yer never slips through the cracks and finds a better deal elsewhere.

••

If you really want to retain your very best Gen Y superstars long enough to grow and develop them, someone has to make concerted efforts to surround them with teaching-style managers, advisers, organizational supporters, and maybe even mentors. The questions every leader and manager should be asking are: What roles can I play in this process? Who are the superstar Gen Yers in my orbit? Will I be that person's teaching-style manager? Career adviser? Organizational supporter? Mentor? What can I do to make it clear to that person that she is the best in her class?

If this person is the future of the company, give her more than the time of day.

CHAPTER TEN

BUILD THE NEXT GENERATION OF LEADERS

I was a good programmer, so my boss asked me if I would be interested in being team leader. I took it because it was a move up, but I was much better at programming than I was at leading. So I spend most of my time programming, and then there is some paperwork I have to fill out every week. I said I would try it out, but I don't think I'm really cut out for leadership.

—*Gen Yer*

They want more status, authority, rewards," said one senior engineer in a major electrical products company. "But they don't want the additional responsibilities of being in management roles. We give a junior engineer the big promotion, make him an engineering supervisor, and he keeps acting like he's just a project engineer. He acts like nothing has changed. They don't step into that role. There is a big leadership gap, especially at those lower levels. How are we supposed to find those people who have sufficient technical skill to be in charge of an engineering project but are also suited for leadership?"

This is the holy grail of retention: identifying and building new leaders. It's not just retaining the best technical talent. Rather, it is retaining those with the best technical ability who are also willing and able to take on leadership responsibilities and helping them step into those roles successfully. How many people have both the technical ability and the desire and ability to lead?

What usually happens is this: Those who are very good at their jobs (those with technical ability) are given more and more work. Over time, they need people to help them. If they are willing and available, these people are given supervisory responsibilities, sometimes informally at first. Eventually they become managers and are taught how to complete the additional paperwork that comes with their managerial responsibilities. But they are rarely taught how to *be* a manager. Instead, they develop their own management styles on an ad hoc basis, struggle, and finally conclude they are not management material. Usually they are stuck, in one organization or another, struggling with management responsibilities that nobody ever really taught them how to handle. They go through their careers thinking, "I'm not a natural leader. I'm a ___." (You fill in the blank: accountant, engineer, doctor, chef.)

Over the years, some business leaders have tried to fight this conundrum by creating technical tracks and manager tracks. The idea is that those who are great technicians can continue growing as technicians, while the "people people" are encouraged to follow the manager track instead. The problem with this strategy is that if an individual doesn't have the technical talent, he will have a lack of credibility when it comes to playing the manager role. Who is going to manage an accountant but an accountant? Who is going to manage a doctor but a doctor? Who is going to manage a chef but a chef?

> Commitment to their work and careers is the first essential piece when it comes to identifying new prospects for leadership roles.

That's why, when you are looking for new leaders, you have to focus first and foremost on those with real technical talent, those who are really good at their jobs. These are the individuals who have demonstrated their commitment to their work and careers. That commitment is the first essential piece when it comes to identifying new prospects for leadership roles.

The problem is, especially among the best Gen Y technical talent, that there are a lot of people who are committed to their work and career but are reluctant to take on supervisory roles. Why? The main reason, according to our research, is that they can see with their own eyes the experience of their own managers and their slightly more advanced peers. What they see is that managers, especially new managers, are often given loads of additional responsibility with very little additional support.

Often when Gen Yers are given their first chance to lead a team or a project, they find themselves managing people—temporarily or longer term—who were their peers the day before. Sometimes those "peers" are the same age, sometimes older, sometimes their friends. Without support and guidance from above, Gen Yers often have a hard time establishing their credibility and getting others to respect their new authority. One Gen Yer explained: "All of a sudden you go from being one of the guys to being the project leader. You are supposed to be in charge, but everybody is looking at you like you are exactly the same person you were before. It's pretty hard to establish your authority in that situation. They are all looking at you like, 'Okay, are you going to start acting like you *think* you are my boss all of a sudden?'" Under these circumstances, new managers are likely to soft-pedal their authority with some people and lean on others disproportionately; to gravitate to friendly faces and avoid unfriendly ones; and to fall back on cliques and ringleaders in order to exercise any power at all. It's true that sometimes Gen Yers thrust into leadership roles without support land on their feet. But usually this is a setup for frustration and failure.

Is it true that some people are naturally cut out for leadership while others are not? Maybe. But I think that if natural leaders

> I don't think charisma, passion, enthusiasm, and energy are traits that can be learned. Either you have them or you don't.

really exist, they are extremely rare. Very few people are endowed with that special brand of charisma, passion, infectious enthusiasm, and contagious energy that inspires and motivates people. No organization can afford to wait for those rare natural leaders to come along and fill each supervisory role, especially if they also need to have good technical skills and a proven commitment to their work and career. Frankly, I don't think charisma, passion, enthusiasm, and energy are traits that can be learned. Either you have them or you don't. What is more, I'm absolutely convinced that these "natural leadership" traits are not what most new managers need in order to succeed.

What do new managers need? They need support and guidance in learning and practicing the basics of management.

When you ask a young star to step up and make the transition to a leadership role—at any level—you owe it to that new leader and her team to make sure that she is fully prepared to take on additional responsibilities and authority. Teach new leaders how to do the people work, and then support and guide them in this new role every step of the way:

1. Explain that this new role carries with it real authority, but that it does not award her license, of course, to act like a jerk. It is a huge responsibility that should not be accepted lightly.

2. Spell out for the new leader exactly what her new leadership responsibilities look like. Explain that management entails more than completing some extra paperwork. You have to explain the "people work" in detail. Create standard operating procedures for managing, and teach them to all new leaders. Focus on the basics, like spelling out expectations for every employee who works for

them, following up regularly, tracking performance closely in writing, and holding people accountable.

3. Make sure you formally deputize any new leader, no matter how small the project or how short the duration of the leadership role. Don't just whisper it in the new leader's ear: "I want you to take charge of this project and make sure everyone on the team pulls his weight." You need to announce the new leadership to the whole team, articulate the nature of this person's new authority, and explain the standard operating procedures for management that you have asked the new leader to follow.

4. Check in daily (or every other day) with this new leader. Regularly walk through the standard operating procedures for managing people. Ask about the management challenges she is probably facing. At first, you might want to sit in on the new leader's team meetings and one-on-ones with team members in order to build up this new leader. Do everything you can to reinforce her authority with the team and every individual on the team. But make sure to take every opportunity you can to help the new leader refine and improve her management techniques.

5. Pay close attention every step of the way, and evaluate the new leader in her new role. Some new leaders will practice the basics with great discipline; some won't. Some will be consistent in their application of the basics; some won't. Some will grow comfortable in their new leadership roles; some won't. And some will simply fail in the leadership role. But it turns out that with the right amount of guidance and support, most people who are very good at their jobs and committed to their work and career have the ability to grow into strong competent leaders.

With this kind of sustained low-tech hands-on leadership development effort and constant evaluation, you can develop your future leaders. Who will move along that path and grow into a high-level leader? Don't look for those Gen Yers who are comfortable slapping people down. Don't look for those who love the power. Don't look for the biggest egos or the loudest, most confident voices. Don't be lured by charisma, passion, enthusiasm, and energy.

Look for Gen Yers who love the responsibility and the service. Look for those who consistently practice the basics of management with discipline. Look for those who spend the most time patiently teaching. Look for those who want to lift people up and make them better. They will likely be your future leaders.

● ACKNOWLEDGMENTS

As always, I must thank first and foremost the thousands upon thousands of people who have shared with me and my company the lessons of their own experiences in the workplace since we began our research in 1993. I also thank the many business leaders and managers who have expressed so much confidence in our work over the years.

To the hundreds of thousands who have attended my keynote addresses and seminars over the years, thank you for your kind attention.

My greatest intellectual debt in this book is to the thousands of Gen Yers who have shared so much with me in conversations, interviews, seminar discussions, and e-mails. Your experiences, your perspectives, and your words are what make this book especially valuable. I have so much faith in your generation and your future because I have come to know so many of you.

To the thousands of managers who have participated in our back-to-basics management seminars, you are my management professors—every single one of you. You teach me every day about the real world by letting me help you wrestle with your real management problems. It is an honor working with you. To those managers whose stories appear in this book, I offer my infinite thanks. I've also tried to offer you some anonymity by mixing up some of the less important details.

To my partners in RainmakerThinking, Jeff Coombs and Carolyn Martin, thank you both for your commitment to this enterprise:

Carolyn Martin is a gifted writer, speaker, and trainer and a light in every life she touches. She and I have coauthored two managers' pocket guides on generational difference, including a pocket guide about Generation Y published in 2001. That early work was an important jumping-off point in the research that led to this book. More recently, we coauthored a second edition of *Managing the Generation Mix*, published in 2006. That work also provided important background for this book. Thank you, Carolyn, for your many contributions to my thinking and writing and for your friendship.

Jeff Coombs has been one of my very best friends since we were both sixteen years old and pages in the U.S. House of Representatives. Less than two years after I formed this company and started the research for my first book, Jeff joined me in filing our articles of incorporation with the secretary of state of Connecticut. He has been running the company ever since. Anyone who has ever dealt with RainmakerThinking can attest to Jeff's wonders. He has such a courteous, consistent, meticulous, and diligent approach to everything that nothing ever goes wrong. I make about 115 client visits per year. And about 115 times a year, I am greeted by a client who says, within moments of welcoming me (or welcoming me back) to their organization, "Wow! That Jeff is amazing!" (Jeff *is* amazing!) Sometimes they say, "Jeff worked with me to customize every single detail of your work with us." (He *does* customize every single detail of our work with clients!) Sometimes they say, "I want Jeff." (You can't have him. He's mine!) They almost always say, "Thank Jeff for me." I try to tell Jeff every time. I hope it doesn't seem repetitive to him. But let me say here, again: Thank you Jeff. Thank you, thank you, thank you, ad infinitum.

To Susan Ingraham, our office manager at RainmakerThinking, thank you so much for everything you do every day to make all of our lives so much better and to make our work so much easier and so much better. I am deeply grateful for all of your wonderful contributions.

To my publishers at Jossey-Bass, thank you for your faith in this book. Especially, I want to thank my editor, Rebecca Browning, who acquired this book for Jossey-Bass and, in so doing, expressed her faith in me and my work. Rebecca made it clear to me from the outset that she was going to publish a book about how to manage Generation Y. So I was honored and delighted that she chose me, my research, and my approach as the best in this field. Rebecca has been a steady and reliable and kind commander in this mission. Thank you.

Genoveva Llosa, the editor of my previous book, *It's Okay to Be the Boss*, took on the job of getting my too-long manuscript pared down to a manageable size. Who else could I possibly trust with such a mission? Because Genoveva was such a rigorous and thorough editor for my last book, I knew she would trim this book with the care of a surgeon. Thank you, Genoveva. I believe you've done it again.

When it comes to Susan Rabiner, agent for both my wife, Debby, and for me, there is no praise high enough. Susan has taught us everything we know about writing and publishing books. The funny thing is that Susan and her husband, Al Fortunato, gave away the goods about how to write and publish books in their book *Thinking Like Your Editor*. Theirs is *the* book on getting nonfiction work published. Still, even with all her secrets revealed in a book, the greatest favor I could give to an author is a thirty-minute conversation with Susan. My world has been turned upside down more than once after a thirty-minute conversation with Susan, always for the better. That's not just because everyone in publishing knows Susan and respects her judgment but because she has an amazing gift: if there is a great book to be written, she sees it. If she doesn't see it, it's probably not there. But if there is a great book in there, Susan brings out the very best in her authors so they can bring the very best out in our books. (I think she might know magic.)

To my family and friends, I owe my deep and loving thanks. Special thanks to my parents, Henry and Norma Tulgan, for raising me and for being among my very closest friends to this day. I treasure the time we spend together. Thanks to my parents in-law, Julie and Paul Applegate; my nieces and nephews (from oldest to youngest): Elisa, Joseph, Perry, Erin, Frances, and Eli; my sister, Ronna, and my brother, Jim; my sister in-law, Tanya, and my brothers in-law, Shan and Tom. I love every one of you very, very much.

Also special thanks to Frances, my niece, whom I will always love and regard as if she were my own child. Frances, helping take care of you has been one of the greatest joys of my life. There is nothing I wouldn't do for you.

Finally, I reserve my deepest and most profound thanks always for my wife, Debby Applegate. In 2007, Debby won the Pulitzer Prize for Biography for her book *The Most Famous Man in America: The Biography of Henry Ward Beecher*. How many writers have a Pulitzer Prize–winning author making line-by-line notes throughout their manuscript? I am so grateful to have had your world-class talent focused on making my book so much better. Thank you, Debby, for giving me your diligent and valuable help. Before Debby won the big prize, I bragged so much about her book that people must have thought I was insufferably uxorious. Now people believe me because Debby has become a literary celebrity. I have taken to joking that we have different last names because I kept my maiden name. After twenty-three years together, I remain awestruck by Debby's gifts as a historian, biographer, story-teller, and writer. Mostly I remain awestruck by who Debby is as a person. She must be one of the strongest and most genuine people ever to walk this planet. I am so blessed to have her as my constant adviser, my toughest critic, and my closest collaborator. Debby is the love of my life, my best friend, my smartest friend, my partner in all things, half of my soul, owner of my heart, and the person without whom I would cease to be. Thank you, my love.

ABOUT THE AUTHOR

B ruce Tulgan is an adviser to business leaders around the world and a sought-after speaker and seminar leader. He is the founder of RainmakerThinking, a management training firm, and the author of the classic *Managing Generation X* as well as *It's Okay to Be the Boss, Winning the Talent Wars,* and eleven Manager's Pocket Guides (HRD Press). His work has been the subject of thousands of news stories around the world. He has written for numerous publications, including the *New York Times, USA Today,* the *Harvard Business Review,* and *Human Resources.* Tulgan also holds a fourth-degree black belt in classical Okinawan Uechi Ryu Karate. He lives with his wife, Dr. Debby Applegate, winner of the 2007 Pulitzer Prize for Biography for her book *The Most Famous Man in America.* Bruce can be reached by e-mail at brucet@rainmakerthinking.com. His V-log is available monthly for free at www.rainmakerthinking.com.

● INDEX